THE HERITAGE OF QATAR

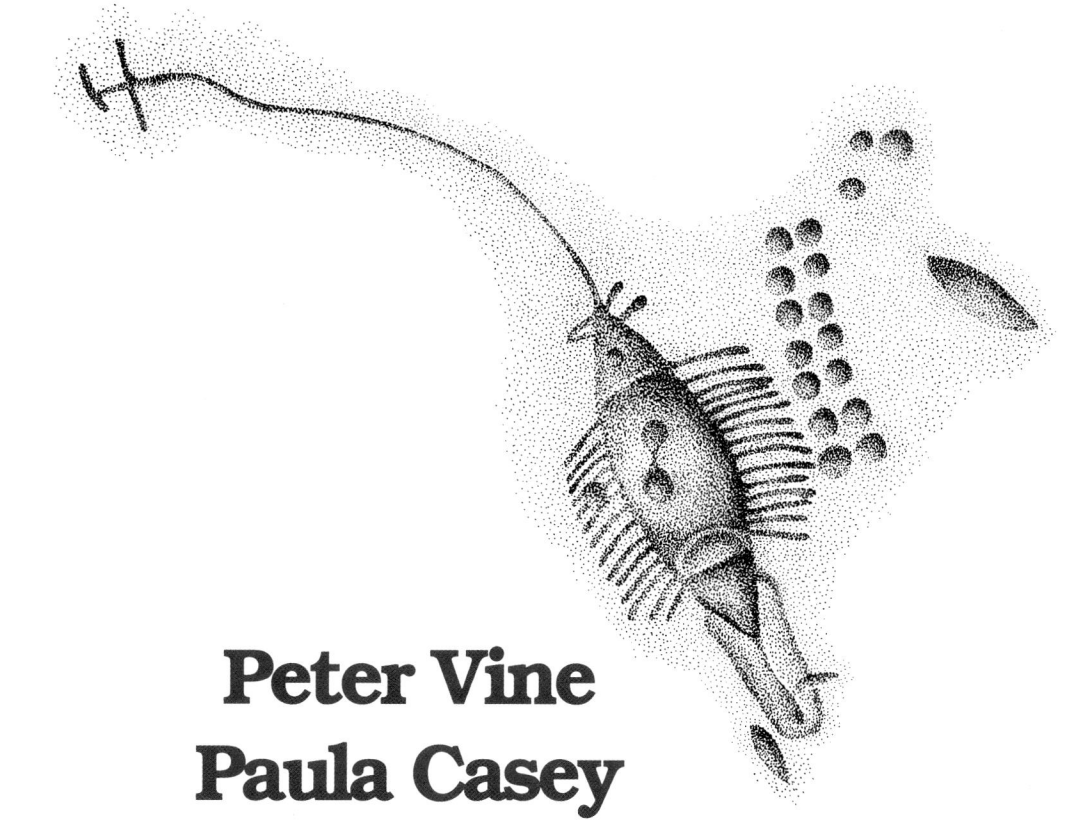

Peter Vine
Paula Casey

IMMEL
Publishing

© 1992 Text: Peter Vine & Paula Casey
© 1992 Artwork: IMMEL PUBLISHING
© 1992 Photographs: individual photographers

All rights reserved. No part of this publication may be reproduced, stored in a retrieval system or transmitted in any form or by any means, electronic, mechanical, photocopying, recording or otherwise, without prior permission of the copyright holder.

Phototypeset in Times Roman by
Datapage International, Dublin and
Icon Publications Ltd, Kelso, Scotland

Designed by
Jane Stark, Connemara Graphics, Ireland

IMMEL Publishing Limited
20 Berkeley Street
Berkeley Square
London W1X 5AE

Telephone: 071-491 1799
Fax: 071-493 5524

British Library Cataloguing in Publication Data

Vine, Peter
 The heritage of Qatar
 I. Title II. Casey, Paula
 953.63

ISBN 0 907151 50 7

Printed in Hong Kong
by Paramount Printing Group Ltd

The contribution of the following individuals and agencies is gratefully acknowledged:

PHOTOGRAPHY

R. M. Abdu

William Beniston

Arab Gulf States Folklore Centre

Department of Tourism and Antiquities

Ministry of Information

Qatar Arts Society

DESIGN AND ILLUSTRATION

Jane Stark

CONTENTS

Foreword
7

History and Traditions
11

Natural History
67

Art and Artists
107

Modern Qatar
131

Bibliography
156

Acknowledgements
157

Index
159

Vine

Foreword

The State of Qatar, covering 11,437 square kilometres, occupies a prominent position in the Arabian Gulf. Surrounded on three sides by its richly productive waters the country has strong historical, cultural and traditional ties to the sea. In times past its waters were heavily fished by pearl-divers whose courage and perseverance earned universal respect from all who encountered them. Indeed, Qatar's pearling history has left a rich legacy of skills, stories, music, art and poetry which helps to create in Qataris a particular pride in the achievements and exploits of their forbears. Qatar also enjoys a land link to mainland Arabia and has thus played an active role in the history and achievements of its desert people. The combination of these two traditions, one tied to the sea and the other to the desert help to create the unique character of Qatar.

The discovery and exploitation of Qatar's hydrocarbon resources has helped to provide its people with greatly improved facilities in all fields, from health and education to employment and business opportunities. Along with other members of the Gulf Cooperation Council, the State of Qatar has been striving to achieve progress in all these important fields without compromising its strong moral and religious heritage. At times this can be a difficult act to play, but we overcame this, guided with great wisdom and diplomacy by our Emir H.H.Sheikh Khalifa Bin Hamad Al-Thani, throughout this period of rapid development and progress. At all times Sheikh Khalifa has underlined the great importance of respect for our culture and traditions and the upholding of our Islamic faith. We also enjoy the guidance and leadership of H.H. Sheikh Hamad bin Khalifa Al-Thani, Heir Apparent and Minister of Defence. Qatar's success in improving regional cooperation and stability, particularly during the recent difficult period, owes much to the calm and caring leadership of these statesmen.

Pride in our history and culture as well as in our modern development and the achievements of our people is thus a natural aspect of our nationhood. Nevertheless we remain aware that on the world stage Qatar is a small country which may not be well known to people who have not been fortunate enough to have visited it. We are also acutely aware that many who do come to Qatar do so for relatively brief visits. Whilst the Ministry of Information and Culture has developed some excellent interpretative centres, including a very fine National Museum where visitors may learn something of the flavour of Qatar's history and traditions, we are also aware of the need to disseminate more information about our country, and I am particularly pleased that the present publication has been so well researched and so beautifully produced. In this fascinating book the authors explore Qatar in all its facets: archaeological, historical, environmental, traditional, cultural, developmental and modern. It is clear from their incisive text and revealing photography that they have captured some of the unique qualities with which those of us who have been born and lived here all our lives identify. It is thus a book which will be welcomed by Qataris themselves as well as by our neighbours, visitors and friends who seek to learn more about our country.

I finally commend the authors for their efforts to produce this book in such a way that makes it one of the best on Qatar so far.

H.E. Sheikh Hamad Bin Suhaim Al-Thani
Minister of Information and Culture

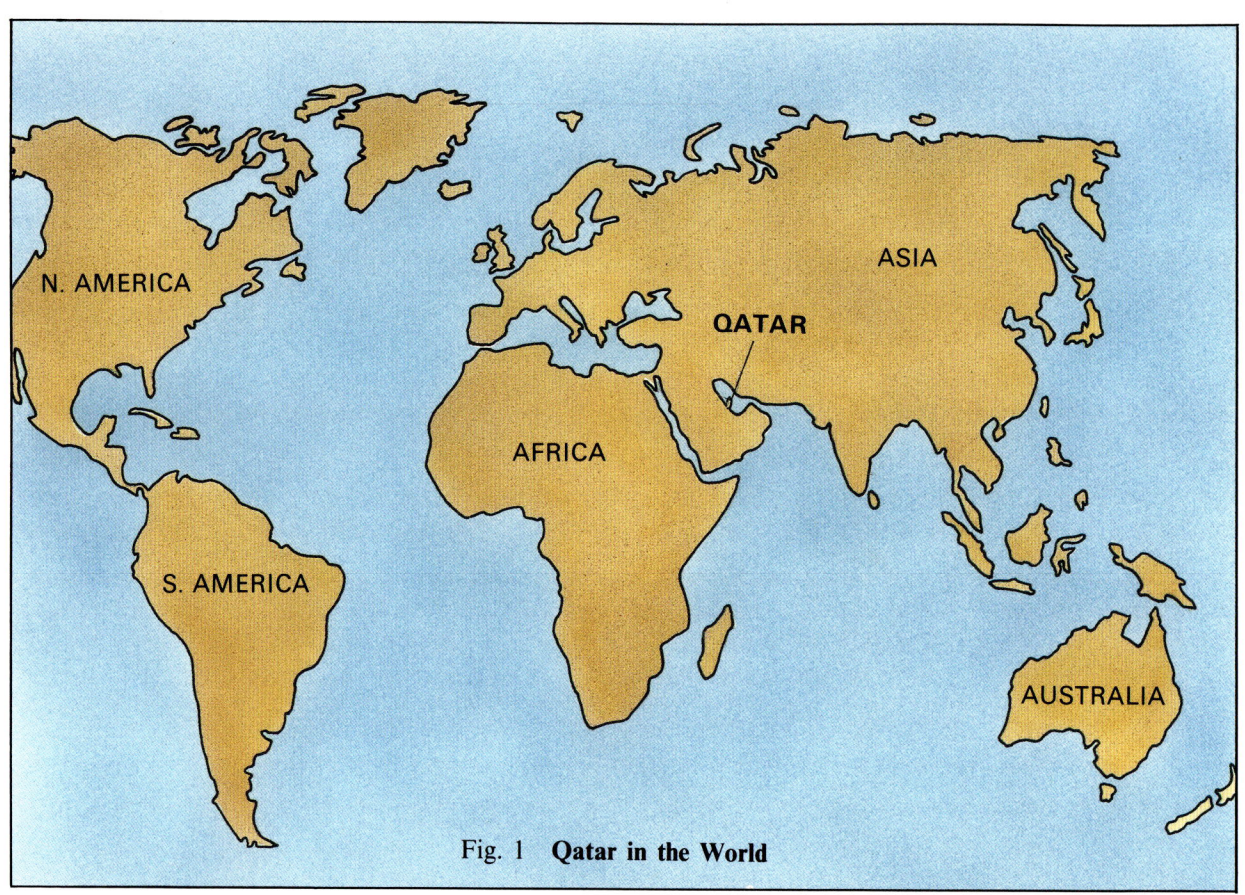

Fig. 1 **Qatar in the World**

Fig. 2 **Qatar in the Arabian Gulf**

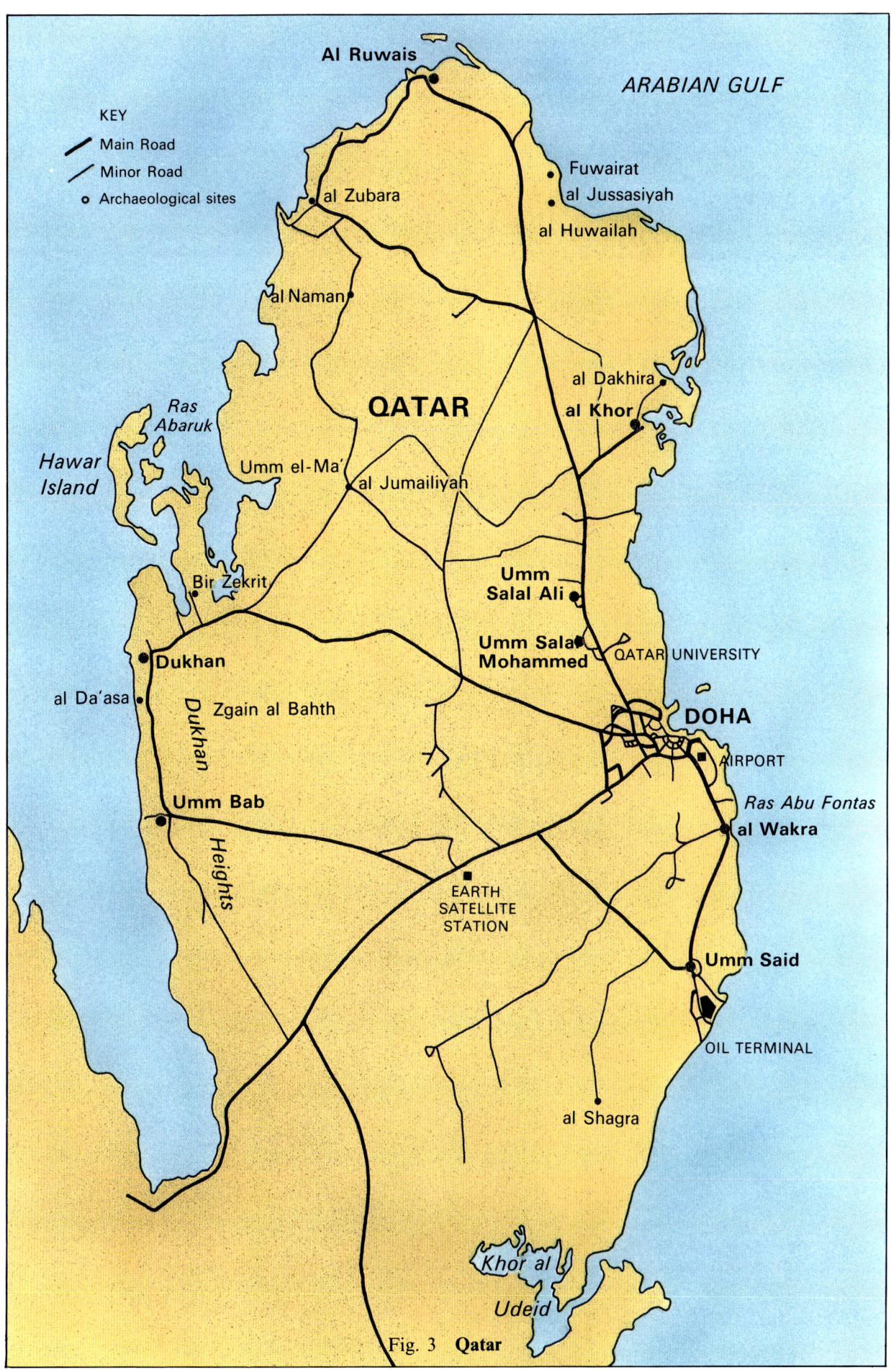

Fig. 3 **Qatar**

HISTORY AND TRADITIONS

History and Traditions

Earliest signs of Man

The relationship between Man and Qatar probably began in the springtime of civilisation, somewhere around 8000 BC. Although there is no geological reason why this stony peninsula jutting out like a splayed thumb into the warm waters of the Arabian Gulf couldn't have been inhabited forty, fifty, or sixty thousand years ago, many experts now believe that there is no evidence of Palaeolithic Man ever having lived on the Qatar landmass or even mainland Arabia. Despite the findings of pioneering Danish archaeologists in the 1960's, it is now generally accepted that the oldest flint tools—key indestructible indicators of a human presence—found by the French Archaeological Mission on the edge of an island depression in west Qatar, are characteristic of the later Stone Age or Neolithic period. Similar tools appear in the region of the Levant from the beginning of the 8th millennium BC. Since no dwelling sites have been found contemporary with these old tools nor any organic remains from which a scientific C14 date could be ascertained, and owing to the lack of evidence for a connecting route between these two distant points, it is impossible to say exactly where these early inhabitants of Qatar originated or how they lived their lives.

It has been possible to date to the middle of the 6th millennium BC a site at Shagra, in the south-east of Qatar, which has been designated as the oldest "building" in this area of the Gulf. The site consists of a two-room structure constructed from small slabs of sandstone, dressed or simply stacked. Flints, mostly leaf-shaped pieces and barbed and tanged arrow-heads, were located here, but no pottery was found. Remains of fish and marine molluscs were also very much in evidence, indicating the key role the sea (situated nearby during this period) played in the lives of Shagra's inhabitants.

General view of prehistoric settlement excavation site at Khor Hill. Carbon-14 dating of marine shells and burnt substances recovered from a hearth on Khor hill gave French archaeologists a date of 6,560 B.P., providing clear evidence that the excavations at al Khor date back to the second half of the 5th millenium BC. (*Department of Tourism and Antiquities*).

Opposite: Flint-stone bifacial scraper recovered from excavations at al Khor Hill. The implement is from the Ubaid period, approximately seven thousand years ago. A quite extensive flint "workshop" site was discovered on Khor Hill. (*Department of Tourism and Antiquities*).

Ubaid Period: 5th–4th millennium BC

Approximately 6000 BC Man began to bake clay to make useful and decorative ware: since then no two communities have produced exactly the same kind of pottery. This fact is instrumental in enabling archaeologists to clearly define a period or "culture" from the pottery found at a particular level of excavation. Moreover potsherds, remnants of broken pottery, survive, like gold and stone (but not wood, cloth, leather, parchment, or even copper or silver), for thousands of years. Over a period of time the distinctive pottery of particular "cultures" has been dated through its

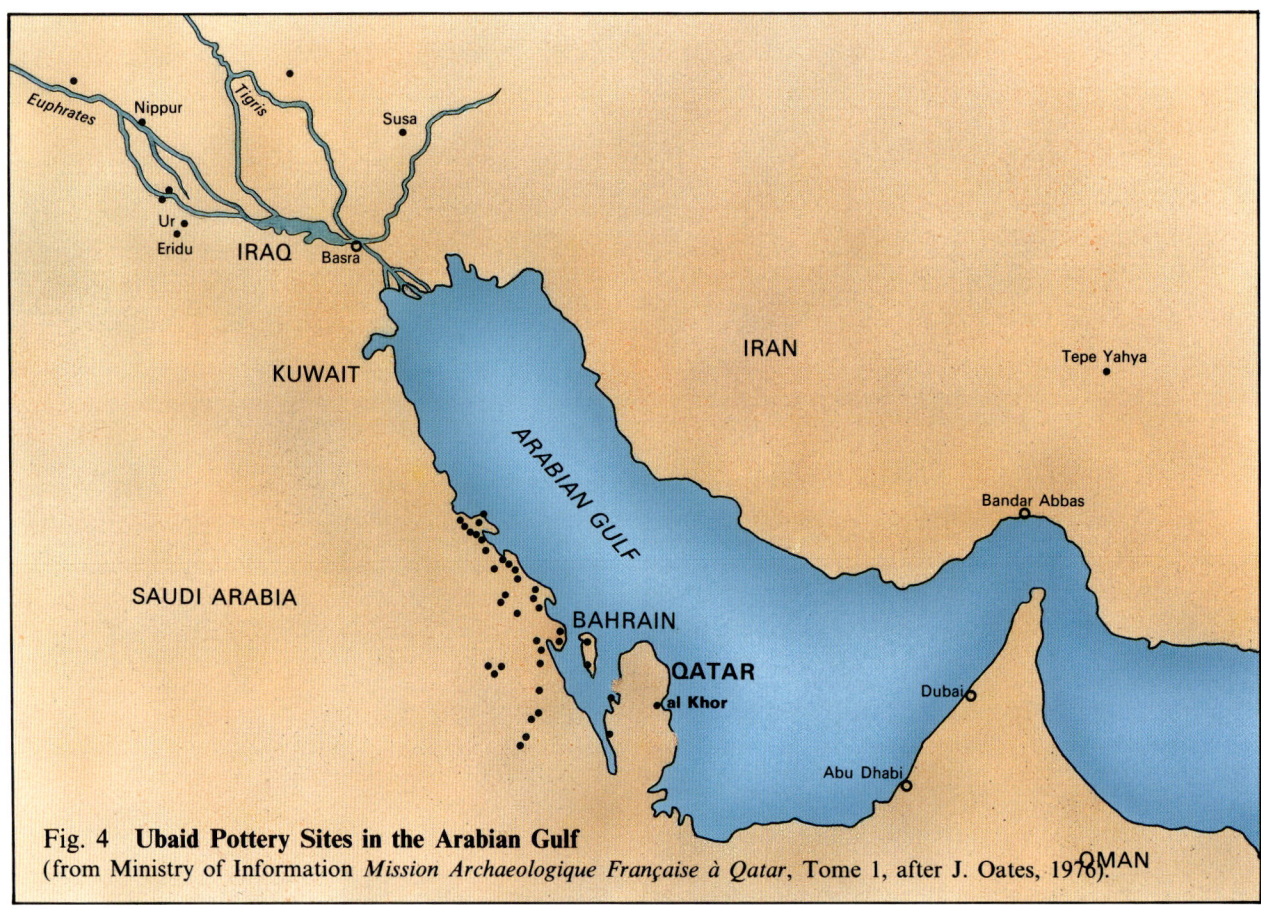

Fig. 4 **Ubaid Pottery Sites in the Arabian Gulf**
(from Ministry of Information *Mission Archaéologique Française à Qatar*, Tome 1, after J. Oates, 1976).

relationship with other objects on the excavated sites. Archaeologists were therefore very excited to find in the Eastern Province of Saudi Arabia, in 1968, examples of a thin, greenish-yellow ware decorated with geometric patterns in dark-brown paint. This pottery was identified as "Al Ubaid", after a small site near Ur, close to the confluence of the Tigris and the Euphrates from which the first agricultural settlers emerged to tame lower Mesopotamia. Pottery of the Ubaid period, very approximately 5th millennium BC, was originally presumed to be confined to Iraq and nearby Syria. However, over forty sites were subsequently located in the Eastern Province, of which five belonging to the late and post Ubaid period were in Qatar.

Al Da'asa in western Qatar was the location of a small encampment on the shores of a sheltered bay where pottery of a late Ubaid 2 or early Ubaid 3 decoration was found. Nearly sixty pits containing burnt stones were uncovered during excavations in 1973, indicating that this was the site of a fish-curing "factory". Stone tools including scrapers (the tool used to clean skins for clothing) points and cutters were found on the site along with querns, a pounder, hammer and grinding-stones amongst other domestic implements, pointing to the cultivation or collection of grain, but no firm evidence of agricultural activity was unearthed. Three small fragments of a coarse red pottery were also found at al Da'asa accompanying the more sophisticated Ubaid ware.

Pottery of Ubaid 3–4 from the latter part of the 5th millennium was discovered by a French archaeological mission at al Khor, on the northeast coast of Qatar, in conjunction with a workshop manufacturing flake tools, including bifacially retouched pieces. The source of the raw material needed for this activity, i.e. large blocks of flint, were situated in the vicinity of this production centre. Nearby a contemporary burial site was excavated, revealing the cremated bones of a young woman who had been interred in a sunken pit—the earliest recorded burial of this period in Qatar. Archaeologists have established that a beach camp existed at al Khor where a variety of fish, particularly seabream, were dried and marine molluscs (including the pearl oyster) were consumed, cooked over fires made from driftwood.

Ubaid pottery was also discovered at three other locations in Qatar: a coastal encampment to the south and on two sites to the north at Bir Zekrit and Ras Abaruk 4. The latter lies on a plateau in the centre of the Ras Abaruk penin-

HISTORY AND TRADITIONS

Top left: Piled stones being unearthed from a burial site on Khor Hill. The fifth millenium grave contained remains of a young woman who had been previously cremated. (*Department of Tourism and Antiquities*).

Top right: Flint-scraper tool from Ubaid period recovered from excavations near al Khor. (*Vine*).

Centre: Finely carved stone arrow-heads attest to the method of hunting employed by Qatar's early settlers who lived here around seven thousand years ago. (*Vine*).

Bottom right: Rim of painted ceramic vessel with part of flange. While very little intact pottery has been discovered at al Khor hill site, the few painted fragments which have been found are clearly Ubaid pottery, well known from other sites in the Gulf, and suggesting that barter took place between settlements strung out around the shores of the Arabian Gulf in this period. (*Department of Tourism and Antiquities*).

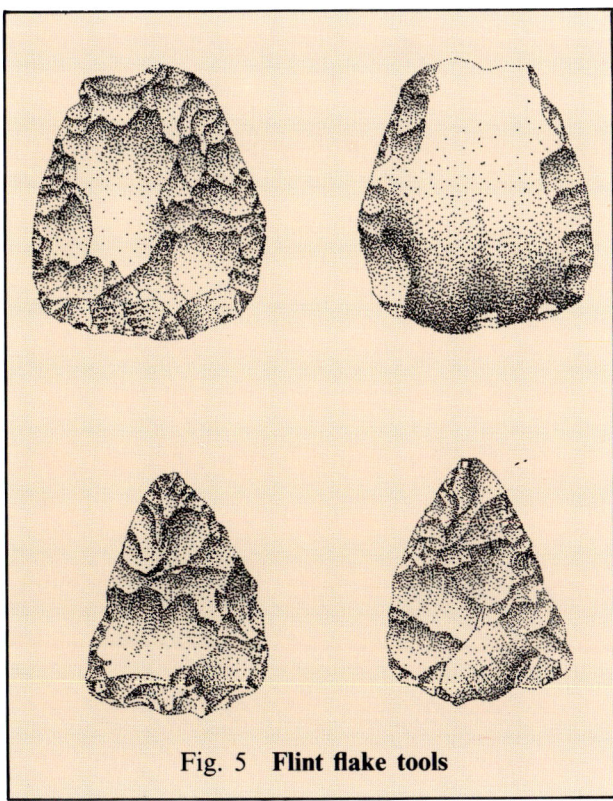

Fig. 5 **Flint flake tools**

HISTORY AND TRADITIONS

sula where sherds from Ubaid 4 and later periods (c.3800 BC) have been found. Beatrice de Cardi (an eminent archaeologist who has worked extensively in the region) suggests that the quantity of flint debris scattered here and the relative paucity of tools (mostly scrapers and cutters) considered with the remains of fish—bones, shells and animal bones, including gazelle and squid, indicates that the encampment had been occupied seasonally by people who had lived off both the sea and the land.

Although links between the Qatar peninsula and Ubaid Mesopotamia to the north existed during quite a long period of time, for the most part contact was of an intermittent and temporary nature as the limited finds at the various sites readily suggests. Available evidence leads archaeologists to believe that all the Ubaid pottery in the Gulf, and probably even the "local" coarse-ware, which only occurs in association with the more elaborate Ubaid form, was made in Sumer, indicating relatively frequent visitations from Sumer to the Gulf by small numbers of people. Pottery was not the only foreign commodity exported to these Qatari settlements during this period. A couple of carnelian beads were unearthed at al Da'asa and several of amazonite from the latter site and Ras Abaruk 4, India being the nearest source of both materials.

Visits were more than likely made by sea since there is a distinct absence of Ubaid material on overland routes to Qatar. A seasonal pattern of exploitation has been suggested in which fishermen or merchants carrying cargoes of pottery, sailed from Mesopotamia, staying at Qatar for relatively short periods of time, possibly returning or continuing on their journey with cargoes of dried fish. However, a question-mark hangs over this scenario. The stone-tools unearthed so far at al Da'asa and the other Ubaid sites are identical with those of the Ubaid period in Arabia and bear no relationship with the tools of southern Mesopotamia; thus causing experts difficulty in explaining why merchants or fishermen from Ur, encamped at al Da'asa, would not have used and discarded some of their own stone-tools or weapons.

Sea-journeys between Sumer and Qatar were entirely possible during this period, having developed as an extension of riverine trade, using the boats, rafts, catamarans and reed vessels which were prevalent both on the Tigris-Euphrates and the Nile. We do know that metal was not used to any great extent in boat-building until late in the 4th millennium so that hulls had to be manufactured from extremely light materials or whole trunks, but it has been shown that similar boats, even *shashahs* made of palm stems, can remain afloat for months, travelling along the coast in stages of 30–50 km.

Mesopotamian influences in the Gulf: 3rd–2nd millennia BC

Sometime in the middle of the 4th millennium Sumerians gathered their scattered settlements into walled cities, teeming urban centres fed by the fertile soil of the Tigris–Euphrates complex, thereby creating the world's oldest civilisation. Four hundred years later Sumerian scribes were compiling the first valuable records by pressing reeds into almost indestructible clay tablets, forming wedge-shaped or cuneiform letters. Around 3050 BC, Menes, the first pharaoh, united Upper and Lower Egypt providing an ideal medium for the magnificent civilisation that was soon to flourish along the Nile. It has been suggested that a link between these two major foci of civilisation, Sumer and Egypt, was effected through the Gulf. South of Qatar, the first definite links with the thriving Sumerian civilisation in the late 4th millennium are found amidst the grave mounds of Jebel Hafit, near al Ain in Abu Dhabi.

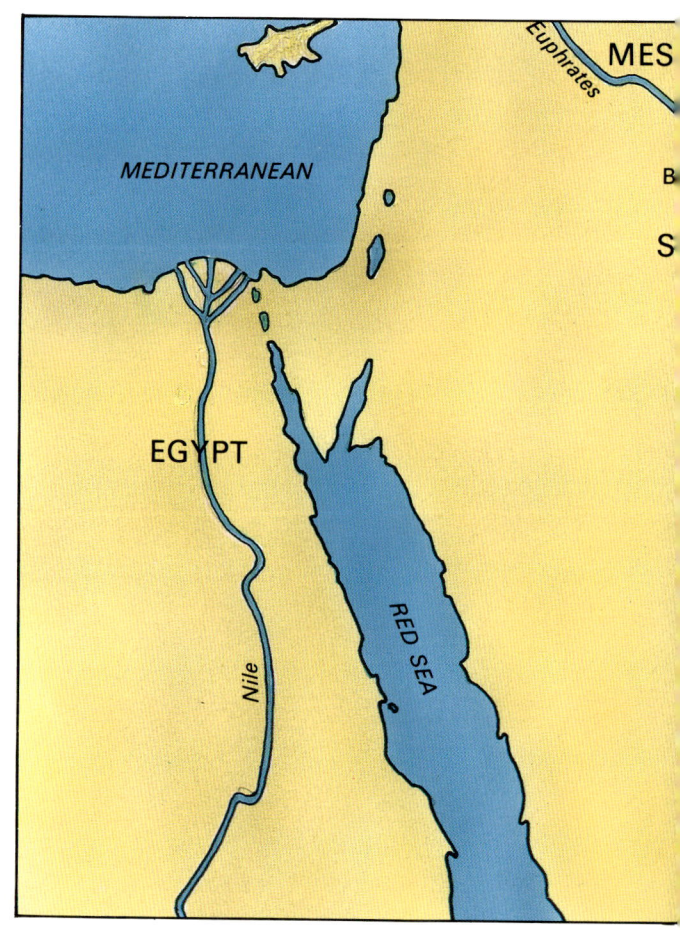

HISTORY AND TRADITIONS

The 3rd and 2nd millennia BC were blessed with blossoming Bronze Age cultures from Mesopotamia to the Indo-Pakistan region. Dynamic Sumerian city-states, intent on extending trading contacts to ensure adequate supplies of much-needed copper, timber, stone and hard-wood, exchanged textiles, resins, oil and silver. Much of this lucrative trade either originated in, or was channelled through, the Arabian Gulf. The discovery in the 19th and early 20th centuries of monumental inscriptions and vast numbers of clay cuneiform tablets in the Mesopotamian region, apart from bringing to light literature of ancient Sumer, revealed much about Gulf trade of the 3rd millennium. The temple archives of Nippur, leading religious centre during the reign of Sargon of Akkad in 2303 BC, were particularly useful. Because temples played an important part in the commercial activity of Sumerian cities, their archives contained a good deal of information on trading patterns. Dilmun, Magan and Meluhha are mentioned on many of the cuneiform tablets from the middle of the 3rd millennium BC concerning the origins and transshipment of the raw materials prized by the Mesopotamians; Magan, in the region of what is now the United Arab Emirates, satisfying much of Sumer's demand for copper. This unique hoard of historical texts has helped archaeologists to interpret extensive finds discovered in numerous excavations along the Arabian shores of the Gulf dating from this period. Despite the paucity of archaeological evidence at present it seems likely that Qatar would have played some role in the thriving 3rd millennium trading activity in the Gulf. Discovery of fragments of Barbar pottery, associated with the Dilmunite civilisation, buried in silt at a depression close to the Neolithic settlement on Ras Abaruk peninsula, certainly supports this case and there is little doubt that this peninsula attracted seasonal migrants since Ubaid times.

Kassite Period: 2nd millennium BC

In Mesopotamia Kassites from the Zagros Mountains assumed power in the middle of the 2nd millennium, filling a vacuum caused by Hittite attacks that ended the reigning dynasty. Kassite Babylonia is seen as the region's first national state of which Dilmun is believed to have formed a part: no longer the independent ritual centre and commercial entrepôt of the preceding period. Kassite presence, or at least Kassite influence, is to be found in Qatar on a small island in the bay of Khor, the only archaeological site attributable to the 2nd millennium. This particular site con-

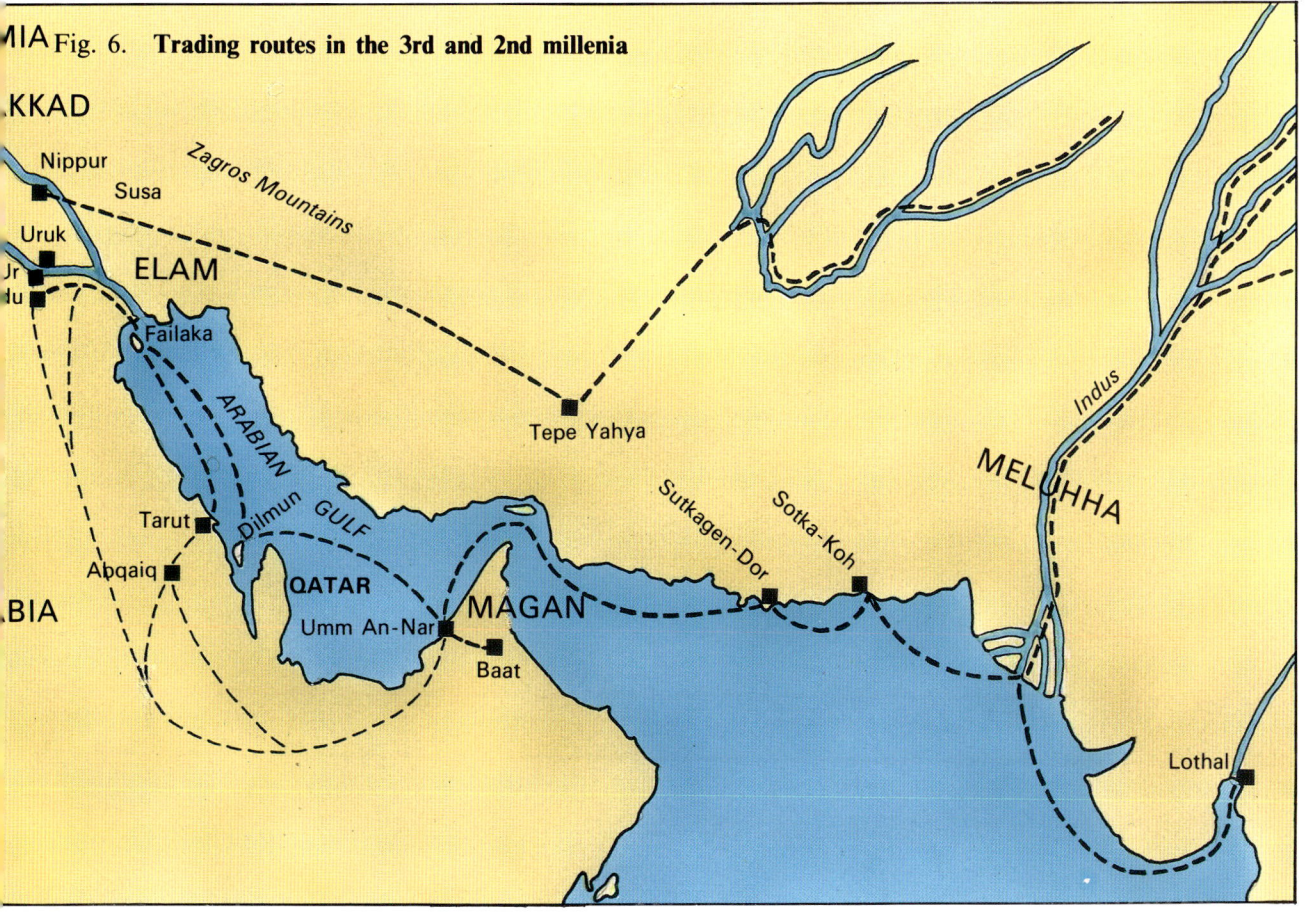

Fig. 6. **Trading routes in the 3rd and 2nd millenia**

HISTORY AND TRADITIONS

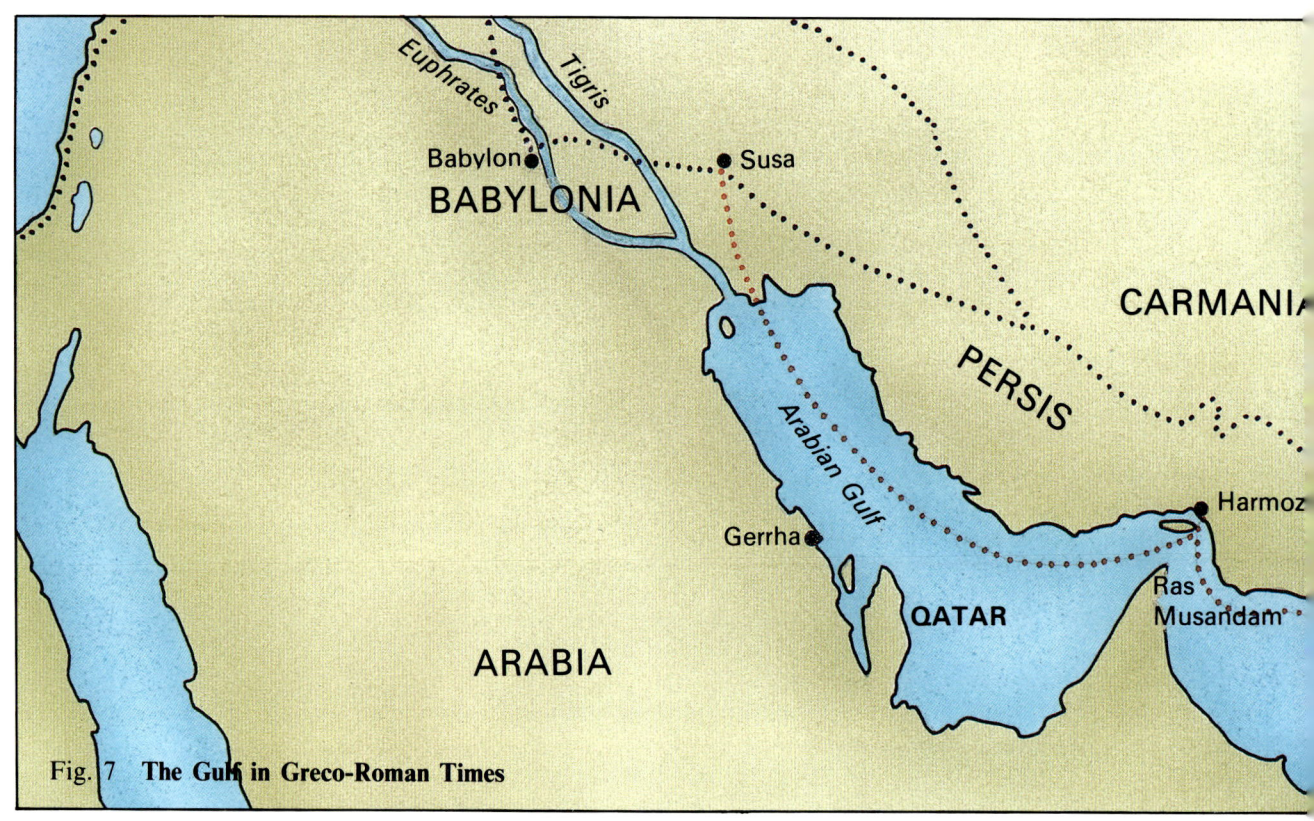

Fig. 7 The Gulf in Greco-Roman Times

sists of a small series of structures visible on the surface and a minor shell midden. Since contents of the midden are largely composed of a single species of sea shell belonging to the Murex family it is presumed that extraction of the mollusc's purple dye was the raison d'être for this settlement. Ceramics found on the Al Khor site are so decidedly Kassite it is believed that they must indicate a very close association with Babylonia of this period. We know from the ancient texts that purple-dyed cloth was much in use in Kassite and post-Kassite Babylonia: following the discovery of this site, it can no longer be assumed that the dye came exclusively from the west.

To date, no evidence of Iron Age settlement has been found on Qatar. Elsewhere on the Arabian peninsula archaeologists have uncovered substantial Iron Age villages, where inhabitants depended on the cultivation of dates and cereals in oases, together with smaller sea-side settlements where shellfish appear to have formed the main food. It is possible that further exploration will provide evidence of Iron Age inhabitants, temporary or otherwise, utilising the rich resources around Qatar's shores.

Greek and Roman Influences

Writing around 170 AD, and using the log of Alexander the Great's Cretan admiral Nearchos as a source of information, Arrian chronicled the fantastic exploits of this legendary Greek hero, five hundred years after the effects of his military campaigns, stretching from Babylonia to India, were felt in the Arabian Gulf. Having conquered Persia in 326 BC and ventured deep into the Indian sub-continent, Alexander approached the coast near present-day Karachi and proceeded to construct a substantial fleet. He himself, travelled back, with much hardship, through Persia, whilst Nearchos sailed the fleet along the coasts of Baluchistan and Persia. On rejoining Alexander at Babylon, Nearchos was asked to explore the Arabian coastline in preparation for a proposed onslaught on Arabia. Three ships were sent to complete this task, each one progressing further and further along the coast, until the entrance to the Gulf at Ras Musandam was reached. The expedition to conquer Arabia, aimed at annexing it as part of Alexander's new empire, was never actually launched since Alexander caught a fever and died three days before the campaign was due to commence, but it is not difficult to picture pearl-fishermen, opening their treasured catch on Qatar's shores, raising their eyes to gaze in wonderment at the great square-sailed Greek ships filling the horizon.

Following his death, Alexander's empire was divided amongst his Macedonian generals, the eastern portion falling to Seleucus Nictator who transferred his capital from Babylon to Seleucia on the west bank of the Tigris. During this period of Seleucid rule, the city of Gerrha, near present

HISTORY AND TRADITIONS

day Dammam on the east coast of Arabia, and quite close to Qatar, became the major centre for caravan and sea trade between Arabia and India. A cairn-field on Qatar's Ras Abaruk peninsula comprising about 100 burials is provisionally dated to the Seleucid era. Such a large number of cairns near the coast suggests quite a sizeable sea-faring community.

Around 140 BC, Parthian rise to power began to interfere with Graeco-Roman trade between Europe and India via the Arabian Gulf, reinforcing the role of the Red Sea as the primary link between Rome and the Orient. Despite the lessening of commercial activity in the Gulf, there is ample archaeological evidence from Qatar for the Graeco-Roman period, particularly at Ras Abaruk. Here stone structures, including a dwelling, a cairn, a hearth and a low mound containing a large quantity of fish-bones were located on an old shoreline overlooking a salt-marsh (sabkha) by a bay to the north-west of the peninsula. Excavation of the dwelling revealed two chambers, linked by a cross-wall, with a third room open to the sea. Provisionally dated to the first few centuries AD, this site was probably a temporary fishing station where periodic landings were made to dry and cure fish. Another site from this period, lying nearby on a fossil beach overlooking sabkha on the Ras Abaruk peninsula, was also probably associated with fish-curing. Pearls and dried fish seem to have been the most important commodities traded from Qatar over a long period of time, the coastal regions being more productive than the barren interior. Pliny the Elder, writing in the mid-first century AD, underlines the difficulties experienced by the nomad "Catharrei" who roamed the interior in constant pursuit of water and grazing for their herds.

Sasanid Empire: 3rd century AD–6th century AD

The Arabian Gulf again took the pre-eminent role in commercial activity between East and West in the 3rd century AD, eclipsing the Red Sea when the Parthians were overthrown in 226 and the second great Persian empire, that of the Sasanids, was established. Cargoes of copper, sandalwood, teak, blackwood and ebony, arriving from the Orient, were exchanged for shipments of purple dye, clothing, wine, pearls, dates, gold and slaves. Qatar may have contributed at least two of these products to Sasanid trade—precious pearls and rich purple dye. Archaeological evidence from this and slightly later periods in Qatar's history has been located from a number of areas. A small settlement about 3km north of Umm el-Ma', on a low stony ridge overlooking the silt basin of Joghbi well, contained pottery which included "Sasanian-Islamic" glazed ware and a fragment of red polished ware made during the 2nd to 3rd centuries AD. Fragments of glass vessels also indicated that the inhabitants of this settlement enjoyed a certain standard of living and may have had external trading contacts.

By the 6th century AD, Iranian Sasanids, the dominant force in the area since early in the 3rd century, were in firm control of the Gulf: Sasanian governors exercising their influence through local rulers. The region of Qatif, Uqair and Qatar was known during this period as al Khatt, which was renowned for Khatti spears imported from India.

The Coming of Islam

Islam, swept the entire Arabian peninsula in the 7th century, overturning pagan deities previously favoured by its inhabitants: Muslim conquests eventually extended an Islamic sphere of influence from Spain to India. The Umayyad dynasty, Damascus-based rulers of an expanding empire, were overthrown in 750 AD by the Abbasids, descendants of the Prophet's uncle. Under the latter a "medieval Islamic theocracy" flowered and prospered, acting as a perfect medium for the cultivation of music, literature, philosophy, mathematics and medicine. Abbasid relocation of

HISTORY AND TRADITIONS

its capital to Baghdad, founded in 762, had political and economic implications for the Gulf: it was inevitable that trade would benefit from the wealthy administrative and commercial centre established there to oversee the empire. Ships carrying goods from India, China and East Africa rode the waters of the Gulf, enriching the littoral communities by payment of dues at the various ports of call. From Arabic sources we learn that in Abbasid Baghdad the demand for pearls was great, stimulating, no doubt, the pearling industry in the rich waters around Qatar.

Except for Oman there is very little written concerning the history of the western shores of the Gulf in the early centuries of Islam. Yaqut al Hamawi, who died in 1229, listed alphabetically in his "Dictionary of Countries" the names of cities and islands in the area, supplementing his own observations with reliable written material from the best available sources. The scanty information transcribed by Yaqut on Qatar has been paraphrased by Serjeant: "*Al-Khatt was, in early Arab times,...... famous for its spears, and the name as a geographical expression still figures in the dhow-masters' pilot books to this day. Yaqut speaks of Qatar as a village (qaryah), and he thinks that rough red woollen cloaks called Qitri with markings on them come from there, despite the slight difference in spelling of Qatar and Qitr. He also cites a verse of the Umayyad poet Jarir, on the famous camels or horses of Qatar for which there was a market there in olden times.*"

Over and above any information we may glean from the early geographers, there is ample archaeological evidence of settlement on the Qatari peninsula in the period in question. For example at Murwab in the Joghbi area, between Zubara and Umm el-Ma', remains of a settlement occupies stony limestone territory, although there are indications that this area was at one time relatively fertile. The settlement, dated to the early Islamic period, comprises almost a 100 small stone-built houses clustered around the fortified palace of a tribal ruler. The masonry is well-preserved and in some instances still stands to a height of about one metre. Surface pottery, which was plentiful, included a tin-glazed ware of the 9th to 11th centuries and a Mesopotamian splashed ware common across the Gulf in the 10th and 11th centuries.

One kilometre north of al Naman, southeast of Zubara, an early Islamic village site with rectangular wall lines, like those at Murwab, lies on a rocky ridge. In one place the stones from earlier buildings have been re-used in a large courtyard building and in tent stands nearby. Except for this intrusion the whole site was probably occupied during the 9th and 10th centuries AD. Pottery noted on the surface included T'ang painted stoneware from China. In many instances archaeological sites from the Islamic period have also shown occupation at a later date: Ruwayda has a large fort and two areas of settlement and the artefacts uncovered there, although predomi-

HISTORY AND TRADITIONS

Opposite: The inland site excavated at Zgain al Bahth, due west of Doha, is from the Islamic period, but exact dating has proved difficult to ascertain. (*Department of Tourism and Antiquities*).

Top right: Murwab represents a turning point in Qatar's history since it is the oldest known fort, going back to the early Islamic period and built on the ruins of an earlier fort destroyed by fire. This large green vase was recovered from the site at Murwab. (*Department of Tourism and Antiquities*).

Centre: Early building on Khor island. (*Department of Tourism and Antiquities*).

Bottom: Excavated remains of an early fort at al Huwailah is from the early Islamic period, situated on Qatar's eastern coast, 28 kms north of al Khor. It was occupied by the al Musallam, members of the Bani Khalid, prior to 1180AH (1766 AD). According to Lorimer, al Huwailah was the principle town of Qatar prior to the rise in importance of al Zubara and Doha. (*Department of Tourism and Antiquities*).

nantly 18th century, indicate that the site had been in occupation from the 10th century onwards.

There is no doubt that the Gulf was a throbbing maritime highway in medieval Islamic times, the extent of this activity surpassed only by recent petroleum-backed economic developments. Archaeological evidence from Qatar, especially the fragments of imported wares, points to active participation in this burgeoning trade which extended as far as China; settled coastal communities wresting from the sea both a livelihood and a commodity in the form of pearls which could be traded far and wide. This phase of mercantile activity in the Gulf culminated in the kingdom of Hormuz in the 15th and 16th centuries.

International influence in the Gulf during the 16th and 17th centuries

The arrival of the Portuguese in the Gulf at the beginning of the 16th century was to change both the balance of power and the pattern of trade in the area. They came not just as traders but as conquerors; Hormuz falling to Albuquerque in 1514. Even though the principal trade routes from East to West had been deflected further south since the Portuguese, with Arab aid, had discovered the sea route to India in 1498, the Gulf was still of major significance to the western powers attempting to establish a foothold there. Hormuz, straddling the entrance to the Gulf, acted as the base from which the Portuguese held sway over the Gulf waters as far as Bahrain throughout the 16th century: their maritime supremacy challenged, albeit unsuccessfully, by the Ottoman Turks who had succeeded in reaching the head of the Gulf overland in 1536.

The task of maintaining control over Indian Ocean routes stretched Portuguese maritime resources to the limit. In 1622 the great Safavi ruler of Persia, Shah Abbas I, allied with the superior naval expertise of Britain, captured Hormuz from the Portuguese. Around this time too the Ya'ariba of Oman, realising that Portuguese power was in decline, began to press very hard, capturing fort after fort from the foreign invader, finally expelling them from Muscat in 1650. Challenges to Portuguese hegemony in the Gulf and trade monopoly to the East had already begun early in the 17th century. On the 31st December 1600 Queen Elizabeth granted the Royal Charter under which the English East India Company was incorporated: the Dutch East India Company was formed in 1602. In contrast to Portuguese commercial activity monopolised by the crown, 17th century European trade in the Gulf was dominated by "merchant adventurers" from England, Holland, and eventually France. By the middle of the 17th century English trade in the Gulf had been overshadowed by that of the Dutch and the English Company gradually assumed a more political role to further its trade

HISTORY AND TRADITIONS

HISTORY AND TRADITIONS

Clockwise, from top left:

Jar from Zubara. (*Department of Tourism and Antiquities*).

Eighteenth century bowl from Zubara. (*Vine*).

Pottery ware from Zubara. (*Vine*).

Grinding implement for making flour for bread. Recovered from house at Zubara. (*Department of Tourism and Antiquities*).

Not all of Zubara's antiquities have been recovered from the buildings themselves. These jars were found in the sea nearby. (*Department of Tourism and Antiquities*).

HISTORY AND TRADITIONS

It is not surprising given the concentration of economic activity on pearling and fishing that most of the settlements to be found in Qatar during this period were coastal ones. The dry and stony interior was the haunt of nomad tribes intent on their eternal search for grazing. Manasir are said to have wandered here as well as Murrah, but the Bani Hajir were not present at the close of the eighteenth century, although they were to migrate to Qatar a few years later: a division of the Naim also migrated at a later date to the peninsula. Along the east coast, fishing villages at Wakra, Bidda' (Doha), Huwailah and Fuwairat had settled populations comprised of various family groups: the Ma'adhid branch of the Al bin Ali and their kinsmen, the Al Bu Quwarah, controlled Fuwairat, the Al Musallam branch of the Bani Khalid, Huwailah.

Pottery ware from Zubara. (*Vine*).

prospects. Following the collapse of Portuguese supremacy at sea and Safavid control on land early in the 18th century, local rulers began the process of reasserting their independence, disturbed only by the brief rule of Nadir Shar in Iran.

The comments of Niebuhr, a pioneering Dane who completed a one-man scientific survey of Arabia in 1765, the rest of his expedition having died tragically along the way, give us an interesting insight into life in Qatar before the upheaval of the late 18th century, a life still centered around the timeless complimentary activities of pearling and fishing. Niebuhr did not in fact visit Qatar himself but collected his valuable information from Arab merchants as well as English sea-captains.

"*Entre les possessions de la tribu Beni Khaled et le pays d'Oman habite une grande tribu arabe Al Musillim, de laquelle dependent les places suivantes: Kattar, Huale, Jusofie et Faraha.......Kattar, un port sur la meme core, vis a vis de l'isle de Bahrein. Les habitants de cette ville payent annuellement as Schech d'Abu Schar (i.e. Bushire) 3,000 Roupies, pour avoir la permission de pecher des perles sur la cote de Bahrein. Il sera encore ci-dessous fait mention de cette ville. Peut-etre ne ressortit-elle pas de la tribu Beni Khaled.*"

Eighteenth century chinaware from Zubara. (*Department of Tourism and Antiquities*).

HISTORY AND TRADITIONS

Depiction of a pearling vessel powered by oarsmen on an isolated outcrop of rock near al Jussasiyah. There are many such rock carvings in Qatar and these are probably around two or three hundred years old, contemporary with the settlements at nearby al Huwailah and al Jussasiyah itself. It appears that occupation of this coastal settlement was interrupted in the eighteenth century AD. (*Vine*).

Rock Art

Qatar has numerous rock-carving localities, but the most extensive site is situated at Jabal al Jussasiyah, a group of limestone jabals rising about 7 metres above the nearby shore a few miles south of Fuwairat.

Rock-carvings at Jabal al Jussasiyah originally came to the notice of Danish archaeologists as far back as 1961, but it wasn't until 1974 that Hans Kapel undertook an extensive investigation and recording of the site: his findings have been published in *Arrayan*, the Qatar National Museum Journal, (no.8, Oct. 1983). Kapel has analysed and categorised almost 900 single figures and compositions into 580 numbered sites. About 141 of these carvings are boat drawings; the rest, primarily "cup-marks" in various sequences of parallel rows and rosettes, have been identified as game boards by Professor Hawkins. Cup-marks shaped into rosettes form the basis of a game known locally as al ailah whereas rows of cup-marks are connected with another board-game—al haloosah (fig. 8). Similar games with minor regional variation are played throughout the world. In Africa al haloosah was known as "mancala" and although mancala-boards have been found engraved on Theban temples dating to 1400 BC, the game was also immensely popular in the coffee-houses of 19th century Egypt.

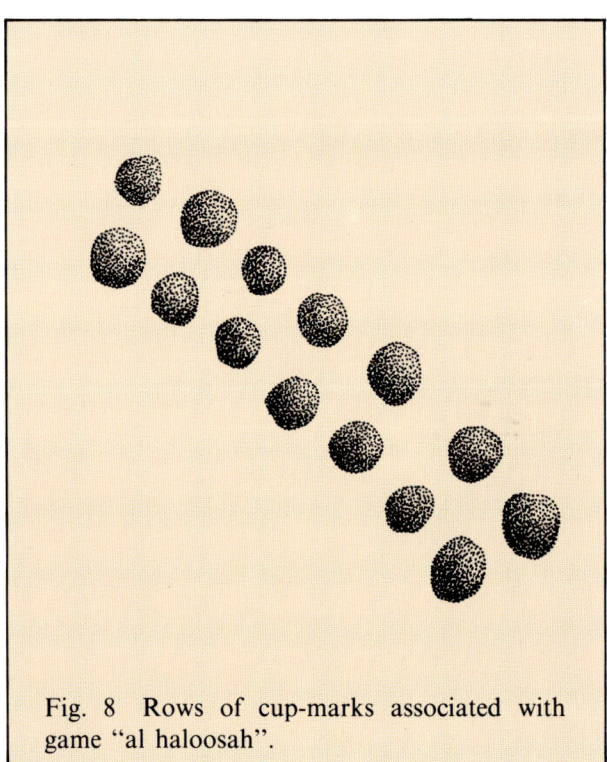

Fig. 8 Rows of cup-marks associated with game "al haloosah".

The boat carvings can be divided into two separate groups based on the techniques used to carve the images and the method of representation chosen by the sculptor: 124 of the boats are carved in bas-relief as seen from above using a system of dots cut with a pointed tool (probably metal) whereas the other 17, all detailed line-cut drawings comprising rows of hammered grooves cut with a pointed metal tool, are depicted in vertical projection. Some of the carvings have been interpreted as many different things, including scorpions and fertility symbols, but it now seems certain that the majority represent sea-going vessels.

Two of the six boats drawn in outline at site 421 (see fig. 9) are worth examining in greater detail. One, a *battil* has the characteristic bow shape and high stern with dog's head projection, the distinctive feature of all *battils* prized for their speed and manoeuvrability in war but also used extensively as pearling boats. In this drawing, seven oars are clearly shown along one side and a large triangular shape, probably intended to represent the sail, is also depicted above the hull. The second illustration is of a *baqqarah* with typical *baqqarah* decoration on the stern post. This type of small craft was once very popular on the Arabian coast but it is now very rare. The pointed sterns and stitched construction of both *battils* and *baqqarahs* place them, along with the *badans* of the Oman coast, in a tradition which is antecedent to early 16th century European influences. These vessels, much in use along the shallow Arabian coast, have a rope system of steering enabling the rudder to be unshipped easily. In a recent paper, William Facey makes the point that since "*stern rudders were developed at some time before the 13th century and after the 10th century AD, when steering oars were still prevalent.... the battil and baqqarah at Jabal al-Jussasiyah cannot therefore be earlier than c1000–1200 AD.*"

In the main group of bas-relief carvings, which is concentrated around site 175 (see fig. 10), all the vessels are pointed at both ends like the *battil* and *baqqarah*; almost every single boat is shown with oars, generally between six and eight on each side, typical of a pearling fleet. The two largest boats shown in fig. 10... from site 175 appear to have steering oars rather than rudders which would seem from the above discussion to indicate a carving-date before 1000–1200 AD: in fact, it is known that this method of steering survived well into the 19th century.

Anchors are often depicted trailing from the boats, both the "Arab" stone anchor and the two-pointed iron "Fisherman's" type. (fig. 11) The latter was considered to be a European introduction leading to the conclusion that the carvings must have been drawn after 1500 AD, however it is now clear that the iron four-pronged grapnel was used on boats at least as early as the 13th century.

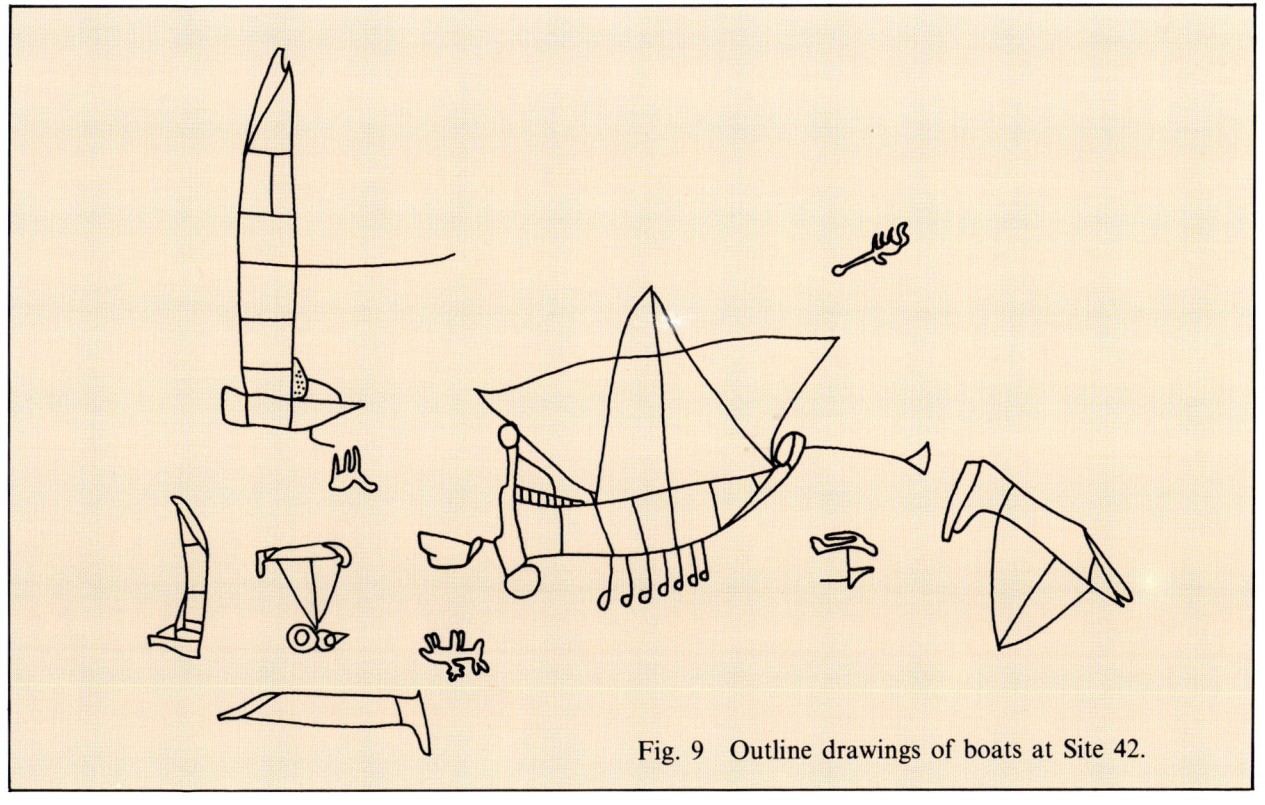

Fig. 9 Outline drawings of boats at Site 42.

HISTORY AND TRADITIONS

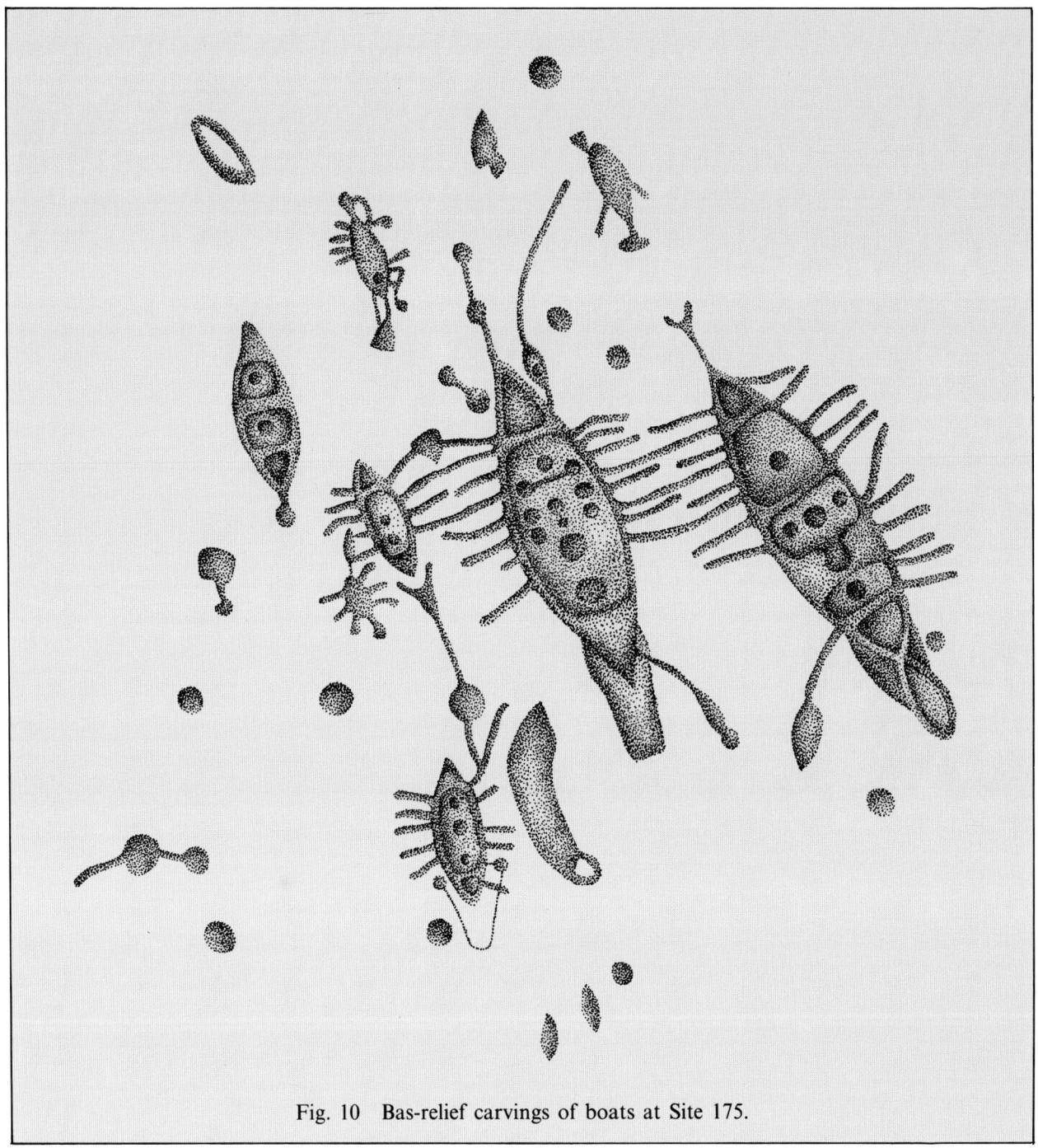

Fig. 10 Bas-relief carvings of boats at Site 175.

There is no firm indication as to whether both types of boat carvings belong to the same period of use of the site, however it is conjectured that the boats shown in plan cover the whole timespan, while those shown in elevation were cut over a shorter period. Unfortunately, the degree of erosion of the carvings is not a reliable indicator of age since certain locations are more exposed to the prevailing winds. Whether the boat carvings and the cup-marks were executed at the same time is another question which, as yet, has not been answered satisfactorily. Since both types of boat carvings are found in considerable numbers interspersed in close proximity to the numerous cup-marks, and some of the boats shown in plan incorporate the exact same type of cup-mark in their design, it is possible that, at the very least, the boat carvings in plan were executed at the same time and by the same people, but for what purpose?

Jabal al Jussasiyah was not always so remote and isolated a site as its modern aspect might indicate: signs of settlement, including an entire village hidden by a layer of sand, are to be found in the neighbourhood. Potsherds found at the base of the jabal bearing the carvings have been dated to the 17th and 18th centuries AD, with a few perhaps as early as 10th–11th century AD.

HISTORY AND TRADITIONS

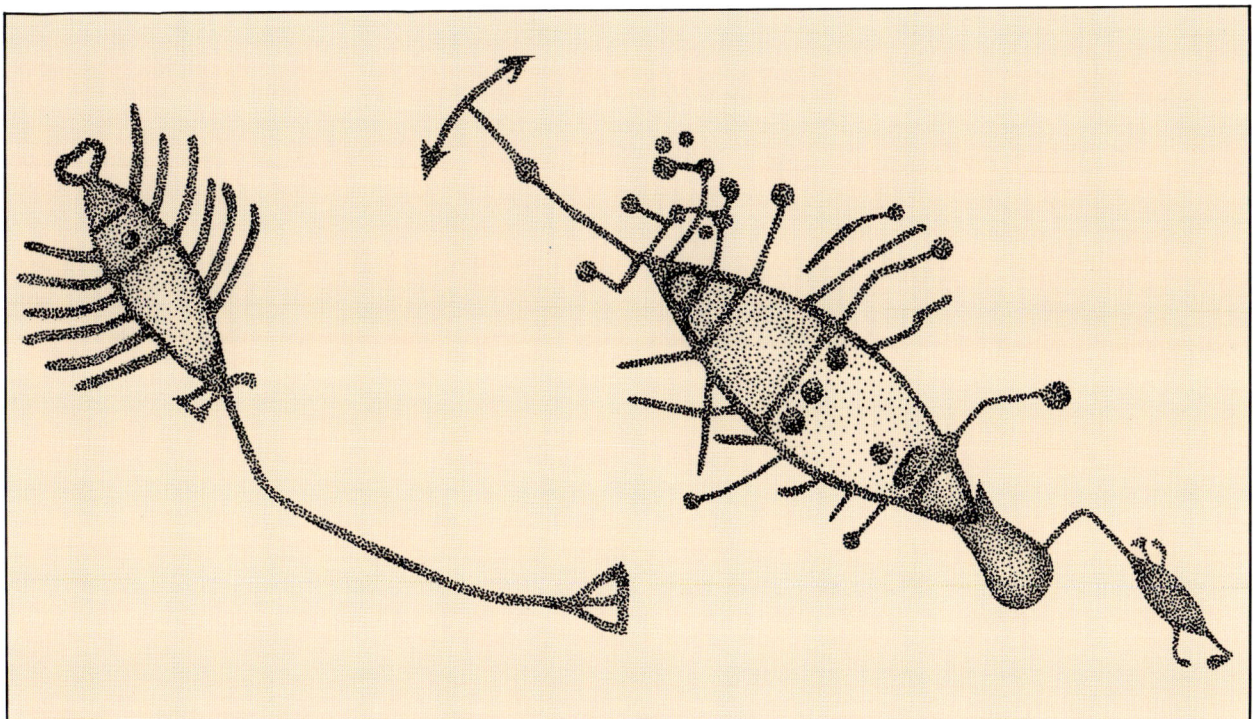

Fig. 11 Two bas-relief carvings showing the two-pointed "Fisherman's" anchor (left) and the "Arab" stone anchor.

Water is available from a number of wells, and relatively favourable conditions for landing boats as well as reasonable grazing is to be found in the area. More significantly, four miles to the southeast are the ruins of al Huwailah, the chief town and major pearling centre on the peninsula before Zubara prospered in the 18th century and Doha assumed supremacy at a later date.

Jabal al Jussasiyah may have been a "seasonal suq" or temporary bazaar, where the pearling boats were restocked with provisions and some trading in pearls took place. If this was the case, large groups of fishermen, pearl divers and merchants would have congregated on the rocks watching for the boats to come in. Whilst keeping vigil, they may have amused themselves by playing board-games and carving familiar boat-shapes. The numbers of people required to accomplish this vast amount of drawings would certainly have been present when al Huwailah was at its peak of activity. If Jabal al Jussasiyah can be said to be contemporary with al Huwailah then the rock carvings would date to c.1600-1800 AD. Alternatively, it may be that such a seasonal suq would not need to act in concert with a major settlement and that the activity at Jabal al Jussasiyah predates al Huwailah. If this is the case, and the rock carvings are a function of this unconnected seasonal activity, then they could be dated to anywhere between the 10th and the 16th centuries AD.

HISTORY AND TRADITIONS

Islamic flasks and a bowl are displayed at Zubara's magnificently preserved fort. (*Vine*).

HISTORY AND TRADITIONS

Clay pipe from Zubara. (*Vine*).

The Siege of Zubara

Shaikh Mohammed bin Abd al Wahhab's espousal of orthodox Islamic doctrines at Uyayna in 1745 inspired the formation of a powerful religious movement which eventually, allied with the Al Saud of al Diriyya in Najd, swept the region. Inevitably, conflict arose with the established powers in the area. Despite fierce opposition from the Bani Khalid, Al Saud encouraged and counseled at all times by Shaikh Abd al Wahhab, were firmly established as rulers in Najd by 1780, but their forces were still not of sufficient strength to engage in open battle with the Bani Khalid and intermittent raids on al Hasa were the order of the day. In 1787 Sulaiman bin Ufaysan, the Saudi general, raided parts of Qatar and, on his way back to al Diriyya, attacked al Uqair.

A great force led by the Saudis and fueled by religious zeal, surged towards al Hasa in 1793 and conquered the stronghold of the Bani Khalid, destroying their fortifications and building new forts inside the original battlements. Zubara at this time gave shelter to the refugees from Saudi occupation in al Hasa. Angered by this support

the Saudi commander, Ibrahim bin Ufaysan, now Governor of al Hasa, sought Abd al Aziz Al Saud's permission to subdue Zubara and its neighbouring settlements. By 1795 he was able to beseige Zubara and conquer other important towns in Qatar, such as al Huwaila, al Jussasiyah and al Ruwayda.

Following the conquest of al Hasa in 1795 the Saudis were the dominant political force in Central and Eastern Arabia although their paramount position did not go unchallenged. Sultan ibn Ahmad of Oman, attracted by the wealth of the islands, declared war against the

29

HISTORY AND TRADITIONS

Top right: A comb and copper flask for kohl or eye-shadow recovered from Zubara's ruins. (*Vine*).

Centre and bottom: Islamic coins from the twelfth century AH (18th century AD) recovered from Zubara. (*Vine*).

Opposite: Islamic graves at Zubara.

Utub of Bahrain in 1799 and, on his second attempt in 1800, succeeded in forcing the Al Khalifa to yield and agree to pay him tribute. But the repudiation of this arrangement the following year provoked further attacks on the island by Oman. Al Khalifa shaikhs thereupon sought and won assistance from the Saudis in return for recognition of Saudi authority and an agreement to pay tribute. However, the Al Khalifa subsequently incurred Saudi displeasure and Saud appointed Abdullah ibn 'Ufaisan as *vakil* over Qatar, Bahrain, and Qatif in 1809 and sent a force to occupy Zubara. Abdullah ibn 'Ufaisan, aided by Rahmah ibn Jabir and a fleet of forty dhows, forced the Al Khalifa to submit in February 1810.

Saiyid Said, Sultan of Muscat and Oman, son of the slain Sultan ibn Ahmad, unwavering in his hatred of the Wahhabi forces who had already made their presence felt in northern Oman and the Batina coast, chose the summer of 1810 to raid Bahrain and sack and burn Zubara, routing the Wahhabi garrison in the process. Zubara's wooden floors, palm-thatched rooves and barasti fencing, set ablaze by burning torches flung by Omanis, did not take long to create an unbearable inferno, causing its inhabitants to flee to their boats, and evacuate the city. But Saud, unwilling to relinquish control in Qatar, reinforced the garrison there. However, he was soon preoccupied with the considerable activity on his western flank: in 1811 the Sultan of Turkey had despatched Muhammad Ali Pasha of Ottoman Egypt to oust Saudi forces from the sacred cities of Mecca and Medina. Later in the same year, capitalising on a reduction in the Saudi garrison, Saiyid Said, helped by some Utub, attacked Bahrain. In the ensuing battle the garrison was overpowered, and Abdullah ibn Ufaisan captured. Saud, distracted by the Egyptian advance, could only free the imprisoned Al Khalifa shaikhs and send them back to Bahrain, having received their promise to pay him tribute. On their return the shaikhs, Salman and Abdulla ibn Ahmad, finding Said in an unassailable position, vowed also to pay tribute to him hoping that their dilemma would be resolved by time. Rahmah ibn Jabir's situation in Qatar was now impossible in the light of the Al Khalifa's return to favour so, abandoning Khor Hassan, he retired to Dammam on the Hasa coast.

In 1816 Al Khalifa again looked to the Saudis and their allies the Qawasim to protect them from Oman. Rahmah, implacable in his hatred of the Al Khalifa, now joined Saiyid Said in an unsuccessful attack on Bahrain and Qatar. His fort at Dammam was subsequently blown up by the Saudis who were disgruntled by his desertion to Oman: Rahmah, accompanied by 500 families, retired to Bushire.

ZUBARA FORT

Zubara fort is situated close to the inland boundary of the ruined city of Zubara. It has been carefully restored and houses a museum displaying various artifacts found in the adjacent settlement. (*Vine*).

HISTORY AND TRADITIONS

HISTORY AND TRADITIONS

Right: Part of an old house on the outskirts of Doha photographed by the author in 1988. Such buildings are rapidly decaying and will soon be all gone except for a few examples restored and conserved by the Department of Tourism and Antiquities. (*Vine*).

Below: Detail of stone wall on old building in Doha emphasises the skills employed in this form of traditional construction. (*Vine*).

British-sponsored General Treaty of Peace 1820

A couple of hundred years had elapsed since the English East India Company had first landed a consignment of goods at the entrance to the Gulf in an attempt to stimulate trade with Persia. Contact with the Arabian shore was not established, however, until very late in the 18th century when British dominance on the north-east coast of India heralded further subjection of that sub-continent and a greater determination to control the transit trade transported through the Gulf by Indian and Arab ships. There is no doubt that the trade of the East Indies Company in the Gulf was declining and running at a loss as the 18th century came to a close. The competition from locally based traders had indeed become tougher, but historians such as Lorimer in his Gazetteer of the Gulf indicated that this decline was due to temporary reasons, particularly piracy. It is generally accepted that attacks on shipping did take place. In the words of Sultan al Qasimi, author of The Myth of Arab Piracy in the Gulf, "*we have to recognise that animosities were rampant on all sides and that instability and internal troubles were the state of affairs in all lands bordering the Gulf*" at this time so that an increase in maritime conflict was somewhat inevitable. Many of the attacks against shipping that ensued were labelled as piracy by the British, adopting an entirely eurocentric approach to the question of legitimate warfare which, in itself, had many grey areas concerning privateering and the rights of neutrals. British officials, ensconced in India, took little trouble to understand the complex web of extended relationships in the Gulf and the fiercely independent nature of the people who lived there. Ignored too was the customary place of the *ghazu* or raid in the everyday life of the indigenous population struggling to eke out the meagre resources of this harsh environment: "piratical" attacks were sometimes nothing more than the *ghazu* carried onto the sea.

It has been claimed that the Company, far from misreading the situation in the Gulf, was deliberately using the protection of shipping merely as an excuse "to employ the force of the Bombay Marine to squash the(ir) competitors"—in particular the Qawasim who had been carrying on a vigorous and profitable trade by sea. Kelly, writing in defence of the Qawasim, comments in his major treatise on Britain and the Persian Gulf that their reputation as the main perpetrators of piracy in the late 18th century "*was largely earned as a result of incidents arising out of their protracted struggles with successive Al Bu Sa'id*

HISTORY AND TRADITIONS

Top left: View from old building across the now deserted village of Umm Suwayjah. Fourteen houses were still standing in 1988, with seven independent majilis buildings and a mosque. (*Vine*).

Bottom left: Mosque at Umm Suwayjah. (*Vine*).

rulers of Muscat". Despite the fact that the constant enmity between the Qawasim and the Omani leaders was the root cause of much trouble at sea, the Bombay Government decided to support the Omanis and strengthen their role at the entrance to the Gulf; at the same time keeping Muscat neutral in the erupting Anglo-French conflict. In 1809 the British fleet launched the attack on Ras al Khaima burning Qawasim dhows and destroying naval stores, all the time careful not to engage Saudi forces. The fleet spent the remainder of January 1810 searching out and destroying dhows even remotely suspected of aggression at sea, however, Qatar, by a stroke of luck, escaped its bellicose attentions.

Since the attack of 1809 had not yielded the desired results and the British were still intent on destroying the Qawasim they tried to persuade the Turco-Egyptian troops who had arrived on the shores of the Gulf late in 1818 to participate in another attack on Ras al Khaima. If the Turks would not comply Bombay hoped to subordinate part of the lower Gulf, assigning Bahrain and Qatar to control from Muscat, even though this would undoubtedly provoke further maritime unrest in the pursuit of independence. In any event Ibrahim Pasha's assistance was not forthcoming. In response to largely unsubstantiated allegations General Sir William Grant Keir led the attack in which Ras al Khaima was destroyed late in 1819, and it was he who actually formulated and concluded the General Treaty of Peace signed by Hasan ibn Rahmah and other shaikhs of the area in January of 1820. Under this pact, to which Bahrain also acceded the following month, the signatories promised to forego all attacks on shipping that were not part of genuine war-like activity between states and the British Residency in the Gulf was authorised to administer its terms, thus formalising British military and political imperium in the Gulf.

Despite the fact that Qatar never actually acceded to the General Treaty of Peace, it was considered by Britain to be bound by its terms. Shortly after the treaty came into operation, the town of Doha was totally destroyed by the Cruiser Vestal on account of several "piracies" alleged to have been committed by the Beni Yas off the coast of Doha. McLeod, Resident in the Persian Gulf, visited the town a short while after the disaster and found that the people had no knowledge of the treaty and its terms under which they were presumed to be bound. Intimidated no doubt by British naval power, McLeod reported however that they were now willing to abide by treaty regulation, thereby coming under British surveillance. The British did not pursue the use of the prescribed Trucial flag under Article 3 of the General Treaty of Peace in Qatar as they did in the lower Gulf; an omission destined to confuse the issue of British control over Qatar in the future.

RAHMAH IBN JABIR

It was from Qatar that one of the Gulf's most eminent "maritime leaders" came. To the British, intent on policing the Gulf in order to advance their own interests, he was a wily pirate and strangely respectful ruffian; to the Utub and ruling Al Khalifas of Bahrain, an erstwhile comrade turned implacable adversary; to the Saudis, both loyal ally and dangerous enemy; to the Persians, a greatly feared rival who eventually sought help and protection; to the Omanis something of an unknown quantity, originally working against their interests, but in the end joining forces with them; to the Jalahima however, a brave and courageous protector, never faltering in his loyalty and his desire to vindicate their rights. Rahmah bin Jabir, son of Shaikh Jabir of the Jalahima hailed from Khor Hassan in Qatar. His bitter dispute with the rest of the Utub appears to have originated from the time of their joint attack upon the Persian-sponsored garrison at Bahrain when the Al Khalifas took over the island and the Jalahimah were squeezed out. Following this event Rahmah, determined to supplant their supremacy both on land and at sea, was relentless in his pursuit of the Utub. In one of many incidents orchestrated by him to achieve this ambition, a small fleet of twenty *batils* enroute from Kuwait to Muscat was captured by Rahmah's vessels as they tried to force their route through his territory, and one of the Shaikh of Kuwait's sons was killed in the fighting.

Intent upon his hostility towards the Utub, Rahmah, always a pragmatist, took care not to anger the British, generally avoiding engagement with their cruisers. Even Lorimer, whose historical research was heavily influenced by a desire to legitimise British influence in the Gulf, was moved to comment: "*The exploits of Rahmah, though in some cases piratical, were performed as a rule under the pretext of lawful warfare; and towards the subjects and officials of the British Government, even at a period when no respect was shown for them by the Qawasim, his conduct was scrupulously correct.....*". However, when in 1809 the British finally decided to mount a frontal attack upon the so-called "pirates" of Ras al Khaima, it wasn't Rahmah's consideration for British shipping that saved him from annihilation. Orders were issued from Bombay to proceed against him on the pretext that several Qasimi vessels which had escaped destruction at Ras al Khaima were thought to be sheltering at Khor Hassan. A compromise was offered: if Rahmah was prepared to promise that he would not harbour the Qawasim then Khor Hassan would be spared. In the end it was agreed by the commanders of the British fleet that an attack on Khor Hassan would be an extremely difficult proposition, especially as, now that the winter *shamal* was blowing, large ships could not approach the place without grave risk to their own safety. The undertaking required by Duncan, Governor of Bombay, they decided could just as easily be secured by the Resident at Bushire. The danger of antagonising Rahmah's Saudi allies had also to be taken into consideration. Eventually the Resident contented himself with sending a letter of "friendly admonition" to the Amir Saud, asking him to prevent Rahmah and his allies from launching attacks.

In the meantime Rahmah's support of a Saudi attack on Bahrain in 1809, usurping the leadership of the Al Khalifa, greatly strengthened his position in Qatar: he was now the most powerful tribal leader on the peninsula. It also gave him the upper hand in his continuous struggle with the Utub at sea: within a short space of time, Rahmah had captured eighteen vessels belonging to the Utub, relieving them of their cargoes. It seemed as if a complete victory was in Rahmah's grasp. But Omani attacks on Bahrain and

Qatar causing the removal of the Saudi garrison and the reinstatement of the Al Khalifas in Bahrain were to put paid to his ambitions for the moment and he retired to Dammam, bloody but unbowed.

Rahmah again saw his opportunity when, in 1816, the Al Khalifa looked to the Saudis and their allies the Qawasim to protect them from an increasingly belligerent Oman. This time Rahmah sided with Oman in the hope that it would be able to defeat the Al Khalifas and their allies. Unfortunately, this Omani attack on Bahrain and Qatar was unsuccessful and Rahmah's fort at Dammam was blown-up by Saudi forces, upset at his desertion to Oman. Rahmah had no choice but to remove himself to Bushire, accompanied by 500 families. Shaikh Muhammad, Governor of Bushire, welcoming the opportunity to extend his own influence within the Gulf, was happy to grant him protection.

Buckingham, in his book "Travels in Assyria" describes an encounter with the aged, but still formidable, Rahmah, biding his time until he could renew his struggle.

"Rahmah bin Jaber's figure presented a meagre trunk, with four lank members, all of them cut and hacked, and pierced with wounds of sabres, spears, and bullets, in every part, to the number perhaps of more than twenty different wounds. He had, besides, a face naturally ferocious and ugly, and now rendered still more so by several scars there, and by the loss of one eye."

Rahmah was eventually given permission to return to Dammam in 1818 by Ibrahim Pasha, conqueror of al Hasa, in gratitude for his assistance to the Turco-Egyptian forces in subduing that province. Still harbouring a deep resentment because of Saudi and Qawasim aid to the Al Khalifa, Rahmah is reported to have attacked twelve of the Qawasim's vessels enroute between Bahrain and Ras al Khaima and to have proffered assistance to the British when, in 1819, they made their decisive move against the Qawasim at Ras al Khaima. Although his fortunes were rapidly declining, Rahmah refused to relinquish his struggle. Forever seeking a powerful ally, he attempted to join with the Persian Governor of Fars who was making plans for an aggressive attack upon Bahrain. At this stage his fighting force was reduced to three vessels and when one of these was sunk on a reef near Bardistan, he abandoned his participation in what was to be one more abortive attack.

Rahmah persisted in his scourge of the Al Khalifa, agreeing briefly to a short-lived peace in 1824. But time was running out for the courageous old warrior: true to his indomitable spirit, he died in 1826 in a typically fiery manner. Locked in fierce combat with a Utub fleet, he realised his meagre forces were about to be defeated so, rather than surrender, he blew up his own ship with himself and his eight year old son on board.

HISTORY AND TRADITIONS

HISTORY AND TRADITIONS

Left and opposite: House of Shaikh Mohammed bin Kha'sim at Umm Salal Mohammed, approximately 18kms north of Doha, was a fortified residence with two towers and a surrounding wall somewhat reminiscent in style to Yemeni architecture. (*Vine*).

Bottom left: Mosque minarette in Umm Salal Mohammed. (*Vine*).

valuable revenue was lost. Captain Hennell, British Resident in the Gulf, formulated the First Maritime Truce in 1832 which outlawed all warfare between 21st of May and 21st of November each year i.e. during the main period of pearl-diving. The truce was so popular it was renewed annually until 1843, when it was extended for a further ten years. It finally became a permanent institution in 1853, leading to the designation of the region as the Trucial Coast. Qatar eventually came under the operation of the Maritime Truce of 1835; and in 1836 the Restrictive Line was prolonged from Sir Bu Nair island by way of Halul so as to pass ten miles north of the furthest tip of the Qatar promontory.

A number of the Bani Yas having emigrated to Khor al Odaid in 1835, British ships visited Doha and Wakra in 1836 and successfully persuaded the inhabitants to take action against the Bani Yas who were reported to be attacking ships off the coast. British vessels, appeared off Doha again early in 1841 in response to continued attacks on shipping. This time a short bombardment was deemed necessary and Jasim bin Jabir Raqraqi's ship was publicly burnt.

Perpetual Maritime Truce: 1832–1853

Livestock-rearing and date-cultivation were important economic activities in certain areas, but the pearl trade continued to be a vital mainstay not only of the Qatar peninsula but of the whole lower Gulf area. The pearl banks begin off Ras Tanura on the Arabian coast to the northwest and spread around the top of Qatar and down the east coast of the peninsula before gradually dissipating off Dubai. Fleets of dhows sailed forth in the early months of the summer manned by men and boys who had left their homes and families to pursue the arduous life on-board the pearling boats. However the pearl season was often disrupted by local disputes so that much

HISTORY AND TRADITIONS

Anglo-Qatari Treaty of 1868

By 1843 Faisal bin Turki had regained control of al Hasa province: his father, Turki bin Abdulla, a cousin of Saud, had been responsible for the revival of Saudi power. Saudi influence was again uppermost in Qatar in 1851 when the main towns such as Doha, Wakra and Fuwairat indicated that they wished to swear allegiance to Faisal who was visiting Qatar at the time. The British Political Resident in the Gulf sent his entire fleet to Bahrain in anticipation of a Saudi attack on the island, and a peace was arranged soon after this intervention in which Mohammed agreed to pay the arrears in annual tribute to the Saudis. The peace was short-lived however as the recalcitrant Mohammed refused to actually pay the *zakat* and arranged attacks on Saudi subjects in Qatar. Preparations were renewed for an attack on Bahrain, but again the British fleet intervened.

Mohammed again refused to pay the *zakat* payments owed to the Saudis on the death of Faisal in 1865.

Mohammed, despite his agreement of 1861, seemed determined to launch a punitive expedition in an attempt to establish his authority over Qatar. According to one version of the events that followed, Qasim bin Mohammed Al Thani travelled to Bahrain to discuss the deportation of a bedouin from Qatar and was

Umm Salal Mohammed is a natural oasis and land adjacent to Shaikh Mohammed's house there is still cultivated. (*Vine*).

subsequently detained. As a result of the controversy that ensued Abu Dhabi and Bahrain launched a devastating attack on Doha and Wakra at the end of that year, razed their buildings to the ground and scattered all their inhabitants. The Saudis registered strong protests against the invasion but the Qataris were otherwise left without aid. In June of 1868 they attacked Bahrain in an attempt to redress their grievances, but although they fought bravely, no clear victory resulted.

The British authorities were acutely aware of the challenge this continuing tension presented to the smooth workings of the Trucial system. However, by the time Col. Pelly arrived in Bahrain in September of 1868, Mohammed had already departed from the island and Ali, his brother, was acting as ruler: it was agreed that all warships would be burnt and compensation paid to the aggrieved parties. Pelly then travelled to Qatar and conferred with a group of local shaikhs gathered at Wakra. He accepted that their attack was retaliatory in nature and eventually obtained redress for them from the Shaikhs of Bahrain and Abu Dhabi. Since Mohammed bin Thani of the

HISTORY AND TRADITIONS

Above: Qatar National Museum. (*Vine*).

Below: The ruined tower at Borj Bazann, situated about one and a half kilometres west of Sh. Mohammed's house at Umm Salal Mohammed, is interpreted as the standing element of a block building similar to the still intact remains of Sh. Mohammed's house which may be the last remaining example of this architectural style in Qatar. (*Vine*).

HISTORY AND TRADITIONS

Right: Sculpted stucco ornamentation typical of old buildings at al Wakra. (*Vine*).

Below: The city of al Wakra contains many sumptuously ornamented houses with decorative painted stucco and plaster. Several such buildings have been preserved by the Department of Tourism and Antiquities. (*Department of Tourism and Antiquities*).

Opposite: House of Ahmed Ali Majid before and after restoration work. (*Department of Tourism and Antiquities*).

Al Ma'adhid, who had moved to Doha after the death of Isa bin Tarif, was the most influential man in the peninsula at this time, it was with him that Pelly negotiated the treaty of 12th September 1868. As a result of this pact Shaikh Mohammed bin Thani pledged not to make war at sea and to use the good offices of the British Resident to settle any differences that might arise between Qatar and Bahrain. The historic agreement makes some mention of tribute, but Lorimer points out that this may have been the sum which was payable by the Shaikh of Bahrain on account of Qatar to the Saudis. This treaty signalled the end of any serious Bahraini claim to Qatar. Mohammed bin Thani's status as leader was further consolidated when Pelly, informing the Qatari people of the agreement in a declaration made on 13th September 1868, stated: "*It is therefore expected that all the Shaikhs and tribes of Guttar should not molest him or his tribesmen.*" In time, through astute leadership and skilful accretion of loyalty from the fiercely independent Bedu, the whole promontory gradually came under the leadership of the Al Thani family.

Ottoman presence: 1871

After the death of Faisal bin Turki in 1865 Saudi influence declined, fuelled by a dispute between his sons Abdulla and Saud. As a result of the vacuum created by their intense rivalry, Turkish occupation forces arrived in Qatif. In July of 1871 a deputation sent by the commander of the Turkish troops to Doha persuaded Qasim, the son of Mohammed bin Thani, Shaikh of Doha

and the most influential man in Qatar, to accept the Turkish flag in defiance of his father's wishes. Qasim was apparently moved by the vulnerability of his position in relation to Bahrain since his Saudi allies had folded in al Hasa. However, his father continued to fly the Arab flag over his own home. The Porte (Turkish government) had already given assurances to Britain that there would be no interference with Bahrain, but claimed that Qatar did not come under this agreement. Britain, faced with the fait accompli of occupation and not wishing to upset the Porte because of European strategic considerations, accepted the de facto Turkish presence, but let it be known by diplomatic means that they emphatically did not recognise Turkish rights to Qatar.

In January 1872 a detachment of 100 Turkish troops and a field gun were landed at Doha, eventually establishing themselves in a fort of the Al Musallam. This garrison was alleged to have been furnished in response to a request from the inhabitants for protection from the bedouin followers of Saud who were attempting to harass the Turkish occupation forces in al Hasa from the Qatar peninsula. The Turkish presence continued in Qatar for the best part of forty years, Qasim skilfully performing a very delicate balancing act between the power of the Ottomans, growing British unease at Turkish encroachment on the Gulf, and continuing challenges to Qatar's sovereignty from Bahrain. Although Qasim's position as the most powerful local shaikh was never in doubt, he deeply resented Turkish infringement in Qatar's internal affairs. Qasim, appointed Qaim-Maqam (Assistant Governor) by the Turks in 1876, was formally appointed Governor in May 1879.

The British, because of the problems inherent in the non-recognition of Turkish rights to Qatar, were constantly faced with difficult decisions on the extent to which they could legitimately enforce the maritime peace in the area. In 1881 in response to threats of an invasion of Bahrain from Qatar by Nasir bin Mubarak, grandson of the deposed Bahraini ruler, Abdulla bin Ahmad, with the assistance of Qasim; and later, to plans on the part of Qasim himself to proceed by sea against raiding parties from the Ajman tribe from Qatif and the Qubaisat section of the Bani Yas; the British authorities in India again considered their position. Since the agreement made in 1868 with Shaikh Qasim's father by which Mohammed undertook not to make war by sea could hardly, on account of its personal character and the assumption of Turkish authority in Doha, be regarded as binding on Qasim, the point was referred to Her Majesty's Government. A directive, issued early in 1882, ordered that *"the Shaikh, though he had accepted the position of an Ottoman dependent on land, should be encouraged to maintain close and direct relations with the officers of the Government of India and to defer to them, as he appears inclined to do, in all matters affecting the peace of the seas"*.

The expulsion of Indian traders, British subjects, from Doha in October 1881 by Qasim, and the subsequent compensation recovered under threat of "instant hostilities" by the British Resident, brought the British and Turkish authorities on a collision course over Qatar. The British, following strenuous representations by the Turks, replied *"that the claims of the Porte to rights of sovereignty over the Qatar coast had never been admitted by Her Majesty's Government"*, and later that: *"the British Government.... were not prepared to waive the rights which they had exercised at intervals, during a long period of years, of dealing directly with the Arab chiefs of the Qatar coast..."*

Internecine strife: 1874–1891

Although Britain rejected a claim from Isa bin Ali of Bahrain concerning the city of Zubara in 1875, Zubara continued to act as a flash-point,

HISTORY AND TRADITIONS

the clashes that arose resulting in the recognition of the rights of the Al Thani. Lorimer recounts that: *"In Sept 1874, after attempts on their part to cross over from Qatar into Bahrain had been foiled by movements of vessels of the Bombay Marine, the Bani Hajir turned their attention to the Naim village of Zubara and, but for the appearance of the 'Hugh Rose' gunboat there, they would probably, notwithstanding a brave resistance by the small summer garrison, have taken the place and obtained possession of boats with which they might have invaded Bahrain. The delay gave the Naim time to return in strength from Bahrain and the pearl banks to Zubara, where they shortly inflicted a decisive defeat upon the Bani Hajir."*

However in Sept 1878, in response to attacks on shipping, Qasim and his son-in-law, Nasir bin Mubarak, besieged Zubara. It's fort and village were destroyed and the Naim surrendered; some emigrating to Bahrain, the others to Doha. The Al Thani and Al Khalifa families subsequently enjoyed a peaceful relationship and, since Nasir bin Mubarak was still proving quarrelsome, Qasim distanced himself somewhat from his former ally. In 1888 the long drawn-out conflict between the Shaikhs of Doha and Abu Dhabi suddenly came to a head. Attacks on shipping by the Bani Yas colony of approximately 200 tribesmen and 30 pearling boats situated at Khor al Odeid brought retaliatory action from Shaikh Zayed of Abu Dhabi and the British. The dissident enclave fled from Odeid to Doha and then to Abu Dhabi, but the damage had already been done. Raids and counter-raids took place and, when a raiding-party of 250 bedouins sent by Shaikh Zayed killed Ali, Qasim's son, in an ambush near Doha, Qasim swooped on the Liwa oasis in reprisal. And still the war continued, the Wali of Basra attempting unsuccessfully to arrange a reconciliation under Turkish arbitration *"for the sake of the Muhammadan religion, common to the disputants, and of the 'latent' sovereignty of the Sultan of Turkey over both, which other powers were seeking to deny."* In 1891 a raiding party from Qatar actually reached a point beyond Abu Dhabi town and succeeded in evading pursuit.

The grand mosque at al Zakhirat (also spelt: al Dhakhira), seven kilometres north-east of al Khor, is dated to 1374 AH. It has recently been restored to its former impressive glory. (*Department of Tourism and Antiquities*).

HISTORY AND TRADITIONS

The museum building at Al Khor is situated in an old fortified residence on the shores of the harbour. (*Vine*).

Shaikh Qasim defeats the Turks at Wajbah in 1893

The relationship between Shaikh Qasim of Doha and the Turkish administration had been deteriorating for some time. Qasim had abandoned Doha for a short period around 1885 so that the ensuing civil unrest would prevent the Turks establishing a customs house as had been suggested by his brother-in-law Mohammed bin Abdel Wahhab, the shaikh of Ghariya; an event which would have seriously reduced his income. Qasim dealt with the challenge to his authority from Ghariya by expelling Mohammed bin Abdel Wahhab and his supporters from Qatar: the chaos engendered by Qasim's absence from Doha persuaded the Turks not to go ahead with their plans. Qasim too was seething at the lack of support he received from the Ottomans when Doha was raided several times by the Manasir and Awamir tribes, and in his battles with Abu Dhabi.

The matter was brought to a head by a visit which the Wali of Basra paid to Qatar in the course of a tour to Hasa. Arriving by land from Hofuf in February of 1893, accompanied by 300 cavalry who had marched from Basra via Kuwait and by a regiment of infantry, he summoned Shaikh Qasim to him at Doha. Fearing for his safety, Qasim refused to visit and instead suggested that the meeting should take place in the desert with a small escort from each side. The Wali declined this request and, negotiations having proved unsuccessful, he decided to resolve the matter by force. On the night of 26th March 1893, Nafiz Pasha attempted to surprise Qasim at Wajbah, twelve miles west of Doha, but the manoeuvre failed dismally and the Turks were routed by Qasim's courageous warriors, eventually retreating to the fort at Doha under cover of the guns on the Turkish vessel "Mirrikh". Doha was subsequently deserted by its inhabitants and Qasim, commandeering the water supply of the town, forced the Wali to negotiate with him for the peaceful passage of the Ottoman cavalry back to al Hasa. In the aftermath the Naqib of Bashra effected a settlement between the Turkish Government and Shaikh Qasim in which, on condition of the arms captured from the Turks being surrendered, Qasim would resign his Qaim-Maqamship in favour of Ahmad his brother, and would receive a free pardon.

The ignominious defeat of the Ottoman army inflicted by Qasim's brave band of desert warriors was a watershed both in the consolidation of Al Thani rule and the emergence of Qatar as an independent state. Despite the conditions of settlement Qasim, now in his eighties, remained the chief decision-maker, although his brother and his sons deputised for him on many occasions: in fact, the Turks continued to treat Qasim as Qaim-Maqam. Qasim eventually retired to the oasis of Bu Hasa, having resigned his Qaim-Maqamship, and his brother Ahmad took care of his responsibilities in Doha. Turkish overlordship, although nominal at this stage, still irked the people of Qatar: but when Shaikh Ahmad approached the British Government on a number of occasions concerning the granting of British protection to himself and his followers, the decision was made to maintain the status quo.

HISTORY AND TRADITIONS

Above: The traditional form of transport for Qataris was either in boats or across land by the "ship of the desert". This watercolour by Margid Hilal recaptures the atmosphere of those days of not so long ago. (*Vine*).

Traditional life

As the 19th century came to a close Qatar's small population was faced with the age-old task of extracting a livelihood from the meagre resources of the dry and stony peninsula. Agricultural activity was mainly pastoral as cultivation was largely confined to the production of very small quantities of dates. Camels and cattle were bred and owned by the bedouin who tended sheep and goats belonging to the settled population. The famed Arab horse was also raised, but mainly for prestige. During the cool winter period entire families and their animals ranged widely and erratically over the tribal territory (*diyar*) in search of pasturage for their flocks. In springtime these different groups began to come together, eventually settling around designated wells to wait out the hot and arid summer. Apart from a little weaving by nomads, the only real industries were fishing and pearling, traditional occupations carried on since time immemorial by the coastal population of Qatar. There is little doubt that both these economic activities had honed the maritime skills of Gulf Arabs and encouraged them to become talented shipbuilders and legendary carriers of seaborne trade. Since the development of steam navigation (a service was initiated between Bombay and Gulf ports in 1862), European steam vessels had come to mo-

Opposite, top: Women's traditional role in Qatar was to look after the home and to take care of domestic tasks. This painting by Qatari female artist Jemila Sherim captures a typical scene within the walls of a Qatari home where the mother brews coffee and her daughters play a local game. (*Qatar Arts Society*).

Opposite, bottom: House of Mohammed Nasrallah in Doha has been restored to preserve the architecture of the early twentieth century in Qatar. (*Department of Tourism and Antiquities*).

nopolise long-distance trade, confining Arab vessels to the transport of goods within the Gulf itself.

These traditional occupations were carried out, at the beginning of the 20th century, against a social and political background which had, as yet, undergone very little change. Although the concept of a unified Qatari nation was rapidly developing, allegiance was still granted to the family, the clan, the tribe and confederacy in that order. Access to the tribal leader was open to every member of the tribe. Islam provided social

HISTORY AND TRADITIONS

47

cohesion against a background of disparate loyalties although tribal customary law coexisted alongside the *shari'a*, the traditional Muslim law. Housing was simple and well suited to the difficult climate: nomads occupied black goat-hair tents whilst the settled population built their homes from sun-dried mud brick; both forms of dwelling conforming in their lay-out to the traditional requirements of hospitality for guests coupled with privacy for family members, especially women. In contrast to the poverty of the general population, wealthy pearl merchants lived in stone houses whose well-appointed majilis' or formal reception rooms were invariably ornamented with decorative painted stucco and plaster. Minimal educational facilities were provided by a few Quranic schools and health care was practically non-existent. Entertainment had a simple and unsophisticated charm, comprising mainly dancing, singing as an extension of a distinctive oral heritage, and coffee-drinking in the environs of tent or house; whilst for sport Qatari's were no different to other Gulf Arabs in their enjoyment of hunting, hawking, and racing both camels and horses.

Finely carved door on old building in Doha. (*Vine*).

HISTORY AND TRADITIONS

The Pearling Industry

As we have already said, it was from the sea that the Qatari population generated much of its income. Pearl-fishing was the economic mainstay of the region, occupying coastal dwellers for much of the long summer season. Traditionally pearl-fishers spent the winter months using their maritime skills to great advantage fishing, carrying goods across the Gulf, or building dhows. Some pearl-divers reverted to a nomadic or semi-nomadic status when the pearl season had ended, spending the winter tending to their herds of animals. However very few nomads actually participated in diving, their main occupation was to act as town guards during the pearling season since most able-bodied men were at sea. An understanding of the full extent of this pearling activity and the primary position it held in Qatar's economy can be gleaned from the statistics compiled by Lorimer for his Gazetteer of the Gulf in 1907. In Qatar in 1907, the total number of boats engaged in pearl-fishing was 817, manned by 12,890 men, giving an average crew per boat of about 16. At this stage the pearling industry was reaching its zenith, average prices having more than doubled since 1877. (The total value of pearls exported from the Gulf in 1905-6 was £1,434,399.) In fact, the largest and most productive of all the pearl banks was situated on the Arabian side of the Gulf. All the banks were zealously guarded against foreigners since they were considered to be for the exclusive use of the tribes inhabiting the Arabian coast. Lorimer recounts that *"in the great bay between Trucial Oman and Qatar the depth of water averages from 10 to 15 fathoms, but there are occasional deep*

Left: Sieves used by pearling merchant. (*Ministry of Information and Culture*).

Right: Net used by pearl diver (*Department of Tourism and Antiquities*).

places of 20 to 23 fathoms and many submarine knolls carrying only 3 to 9: fathoms; the last are the principal scene of pearling operations in this part of the Gulf."

The pearling industry had a social structure all of its own with many key individuals playing vital roles in the successful outcome of the season. The money required to outfit pearling boats with food and equipment for the season and to advance quite considerable sums to divers in order to secure their services and maintain their families while they were at sea was normally borrowed from a class of financier called *mussaqam*, who may in turn have secured loans from wealthy merchants. The *nakhuda* or captain of each pearling boat was, generally speaking, owner of the boat under his command; but sometimes he hired the boat or was simply employed by the boat's owner. Next in importance to the *nakhuda* were the *ghasah* (sing. *ghais*) or divers, followed by the *siyub* (sing. *saib*) or haulers. One or more *radfah* (sing. *radhif*) or extra hands were generally carried to assist the haulers, and sometimes a young *walaid* or apprentice was employed to catch fish, cook, and look after the pipes and coffee. Young boys commenced their apprenticeship around the age of 10, gradually developing all the skills of sailing, navigation, diving and other activities carried out by the pearling crew.

PEARLING

The season for harvesting pearls (*al ghaus*) was subdivided into 3 main periods. Hansiyah began in mid-April and lasted for 40 days; *ghaus al kebir* was the main diving season stretching from the end of May until the first 10 days of September; and the *raddah* took place over the last few days of September into the first two weeks of October. *Sambuqs* were traditionally used as pearling boats but *batils baggarahs* and *shu'ais* were also to be found. Until recently these boats carried neither charts nor compasses but their captains were, nevertheless, extremely adept at locating the pearl banks, guided by the sun and stars; by bearings from the land when in sight; and by the colour and depth of the sea. Some *nakhudas* sailed straight to a particular bank and stayed there until the end of the season whereas others moved from bank to bank. In the choice of location the *nakhuda* was limited by the skill and daring of his divers; 8 fathoms was the normal depth at which the average diver could comfortably work; 12 was probably the limit for most; whereas boats with exceptionally talented divers could work on banks covered by up to 14 fathoms.

The divers' day was long and arduous with little opportunity for rest and food: work began an hour after sunrise and finished an hour before sunset. However exertions on board were alleviated by almost constant singing, clapping and beating of rhythms on *gahlah* or *tabl* coordinated by a *nahham*, the principal singer of the group. Using a shift system, the crew was divided into two groups; one worked while the other sang and clapped in order to entertain themselves and encourage the working shift. The nahham on the larger boats was exempt from physical work and concentrated all his attention on his very important musical duties. The interval between the early morning prayer and the first dive of the day was spent by the crew in opening the oysters collected on the previous day. This operation was invariably completed under the eagle eye of the *nakhuda*, who took charge of the catch: anyone finding a specially good pearl was suitably rewarded. Before the diving began, a very light meal of half a pound of dates and a few cups of coffee was consumed. Then the divers prepared themselves for their underwater work: horn pincers (*fatam*) were clipped onto noses, ears were plugged with cotton-wool or bees wax, and protective tips called (*khabat*) were placed on fingers. Hanging a small bag (*diyin*) around his neck or waist, the diver placed his foot in the noose of a rope (*zaibal*) to which a weight of 10-14lbs was attached and plummetted through the cool water to the bottom of the sea. Holding his breath, the diver attempted to fill his bag with as many oysters as possible. When he could stay down no longer, the diver signalled to his attendant *saib* by jerking a rope (*ida*) around his waist and was immediately pulled up to the surface and his bag of shells emptied. The shells gathered by a *ghais* in a single plunge or *tabbah* generally numbered from 3–20; sometimes however he returned entirely empty-handed. The time occupied by the plunge was usually from 40 to 75 seconds but only a few divers could remain below water for more than one minute. Between dives the ghais usually rested in the water, hanging, in characteristic pose, by a rope over the side of the boat: the same diver made as many as 50 plunges in a day if the weather was clement, but only 10 or 20 if the water was cold.

Diving was always interrupted for the mid-day prayer when coffee was again drunk and a rest taken for about an hour. Following this brief interlude, pearl harvesting continued throughout the afternoon until evening prayers. Although the work was extremely hard, the only real health hazard experienced by the divers were skin diseases and respiratory problems. Despite popular misconceptions, shark attacks were in fact extremely rare, but divers sometimes wore a long white shirt to protect themselves from the stings of the 'devil-fish'. Soon after they had performed their religious duties in the evening, the divers consumed their main meal of fish, rice and dates followed by a little smoking and coffee-drinking, and sometimes even a visit to a nearby boat. Quarrels were rare on the pearling ground, and boats of temporarily hostile tribes were often peacefully anchored side by side on the banks.

Table 1. An inventory of pearling ships and their crews from Qatari ports in 1907. (after Lorimer)

	Number of boats	Number of men
Khor Hassan	20	240
Abu Dhaluf	20	200
Ruwais	?	270
Fuwairat	35	420
Dhakhirah	15	180
Khor Shaqiq (Khor)	80	1200
Sumaismah	50	600
Dha'ain	70	840
Lusail	9	90
Doha	350	6300
Wakrah	150	2550
	817	12890

HISTORY AND TRADITIONS

Qatar's past is closely tied-up with pearling and although commercial pearling no longer takes place from the modern State of Qatar, its older people have fond memories of those days. This re-enactment of a pearling expedition was co-sponsored by the Arab Gulf States Folklore Centre whose headquarters are in Doha. (*AGSFC*).

HISTORY AND TRADITIONS

A painting by Wafaa al Hamed of the Qatar Arts Society brings to life the old pearling days in Qatar.

Trade in pearls

The boats of each district formed a fleet with one of the *nakhudas* appointed before sailing, by the shaikh of the district, as its admiral. His principal duty was to fix the date for the whole fleet to return en masse to port. Any boat, no matter how successful, arriving home before the admiral without an adequate excuse was severely dealt with by the shaikh to whose jurisdiction they belonged. Most crews, however, paid one or more brief visits to port in the course of the season to see their families, to revictual, or to scrape the barnacles from the sides of the boats. On return from the banks the *nakhuda*, if financed by a *musaqqam*, was bound to hand over to his creditor the whole take of pearls, and all the shells brought home, at a rate previously arranged which varied from 15 to 20 per cent below market value. The payment of 80 to 85 per cent of value paid by the *musaqqam* was divided among the owner, *nakhuda*, and crew of the boat. The *nakhuda* however, was not precluded from selling his pearls to a tajir or professional pearl merchant at a higher price, in the event of the *musaqqam* not being willing to pay such a price. The *nakhuda* could then discharge his debt to the *musaqqam*, the owner of the boat would receive one-fifth of the whole; rations were paid for; and the balance was then divided up among the operatives, the *nakhuda* and each *ghais* or diver receiving 3 shares, each *saib* or hauler 2, and each *radhif* or extra hand 1; the *walaid* or apprentice was not entitled to a share. As one might imagine considering the way in which the pearling trade was financed, the pearling industry was governed by stringent customs as to debt, customs which had the force of law and were rigorously enforced by local tribunals.

The *tajir's* business was brought to his door but the *tawwash* or petty merchant had to go in search of his trade, however they both used the same system for measuring and classifying the pearl harvest. Exceptionally large and fine pearls were bought and sold singly, medium pearls were sorted with reference to size by being passed through a series of perforated bowls called *tus* which were made of brass or copper. The ordinary pearl, after being purchased from an operative by size, usually passed from one dealer to another on a more precise kind of estimate based upon weight. The majority of the pearls were exported to Bombay where they were classified for despatch to European and other markets, but some were sent to Baghdad. The pearl trade, as we have already mentioned, prospered as the 20th century dawned, ensuring that the coastal population was at least guaranteed the basics of life, some even growing rich on the trade, but this short-lived prosperity was soon to founder. In this era of oil-sponsored affluence, nostalgic reflection, hankering after a simpler society, often focuses on the more positive aspects of the pearling, forgetting the real hardships, insecurity and deprivations that the pearlers and their families endured.

Boats and boatbuilding.

It is not surprising, considering the extent of pearling activity and the economic importance of fishing and sea trade, that Qataris were accomplished boatbuilders, crafting traditional wooden dhows from imported timber. The term dhow actually encompasses many different types of vessel, distinguished according to the shape of the hull: *baghlah*, *boum*, *sambuq*, *shu'i*, *battil*, *baggarah*, and *jalibut* rode the waters of the Gulf, whilst the *huri* and *shashah* were used for inshore fishing.

The design of the *baghlah*, encompassing a high poop deck and quarter galleries, its elaborately carved transom stern pierced by five windows, owed much to Portuguese influence on Arab boat building after the 16th century. The *baghlah*, a magnificent and stately craft up to 135 feet long, its stem curved and topped with a distinctive bollard-shaped figure-head, was the traditional ocean-going vessel of the Gulf until its paramount position was supplanted, in the middle of the 20th century, by the double-ended *boum* which retains its hull shape from the pre-Portuguese era. The *boum*, ranging in tonnage from 74 to 400 tons and in length from 50 to 120 feet, is readily distinguished by its high, straight stem-post built out into a kind of planked bowsprit which is normally decorated at its tip with a simple design in black and white. The *sambuq*, its graceful lines augmented by a low, curved, scimitar-shaped stem piece and high square stern, is an extremely versatile craft and, much employed in fishing and pearling and even deep-sea trading in the early part of this century.

Boat building was an essential part of Qatari life with the boat-builder highly regarded within the community. This craft has not quite died in Qatar where recent efforts to revive it have centred on projects to construct new dhows, booms and other traditional vessels. Life in a Qatari boatyard is depicted here by local artist Yousef al Sherif. (*Qatar Arts Society*).

HISTORY AND TRADITIONS

Doha in the pearling era. (*Sultan al-Ghanem*).

As a result this particular vessel varied enormously in size, from 20 to as much as 150 tons. The *shu'i* was almost identical to the smaller *sambuqs*, although it usually had a straight stem-piece: motorised *shu'i*'s and *sambuqs* are still very popular today as fishing and trading vessels. The *jalibut*, about 50 feet in length and easily recognised by its vertical bow, was also used extensively as a pearling vessel in the Gulf. It too, is square-sterned but of a much more functional design, lacking the elegance and beauty of the *sambuq*. The speedy double-ended *battil*, lying long and low in the water was used both as a coastal trading vessel and in warfare. It was probably the most unusual of Arab vessels with a stem-piece carved like a rounded club or fiddle head and a high "dog's head" stern post. The *baggarah* was also double-ended and it too used the rope system of steering but, unlike the *battil*, its stem-piece continued in a straight line, painted and carved, whilst the high stern-post was without any distinctive projections.

Attempts are being made to revive the ancient skills involved in boatbuilding in present day Qatar. Shell construction in which planks are

HISTORY AND TRADITIONS

fitted first and the ribs later is the traditional Arab method of boat building, standing in direct contrast to the European practice of fitting the ribs before the planking is laid. Although, as we have seen, the design of some of the boats has been heavily influenced by Europe, traditional boat building methods hark back to the pre-Portuguese period when wooden vessels were sewn together with coconut fibre. Boats are all carvel-built with the planks laid edge to edge, master craftsmen achieving remarkable accuracy working by eye and experience, entirely unaided by any plans or drawings. Templates are, however, used to determine the shape of the hull planking. Traditionally, the tools used in boat building are very basic, hammer, saw, adze, bow-drill, chisel, plane and caulking iron are all that the tool-kit contains; and the stark contrast between the simplicity of building techniques and the sophistication and grace of the finished product is a source of constant wonder. Caulking of the hull was traditionally effected with a mixture of fibre or raw cotton impregnated with fish, coconut or simsin oil. The hull below the waterline was insulated against the destructive effects of the teredo worm by a coating made by boiling oil, animal fat or resin with whitewash or lime. Above the waterline fish oil or vegetable oil was painted onto the teak hull bringing out the wood's dark glossy characteristics.

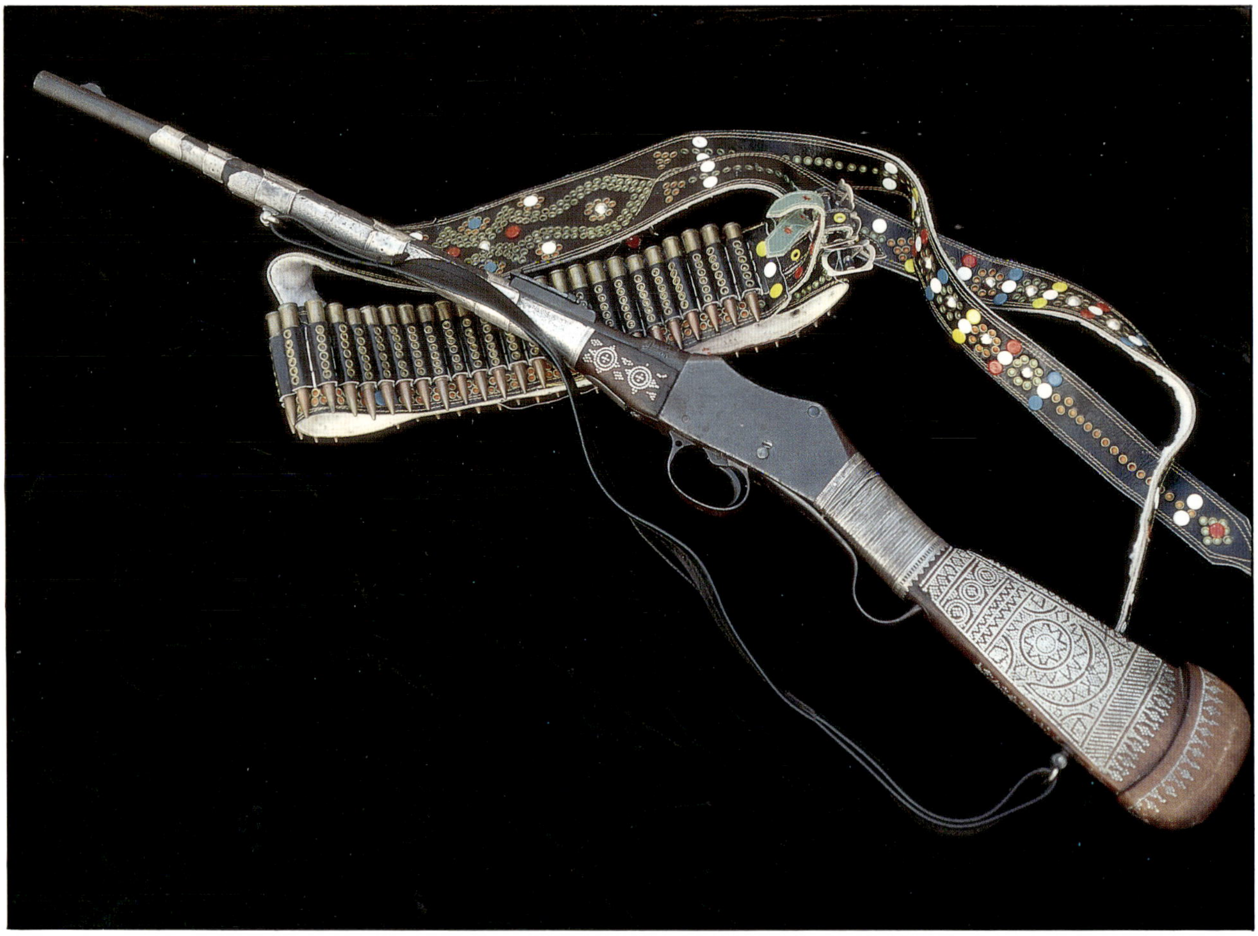

HISTORY AND TRADITIONS

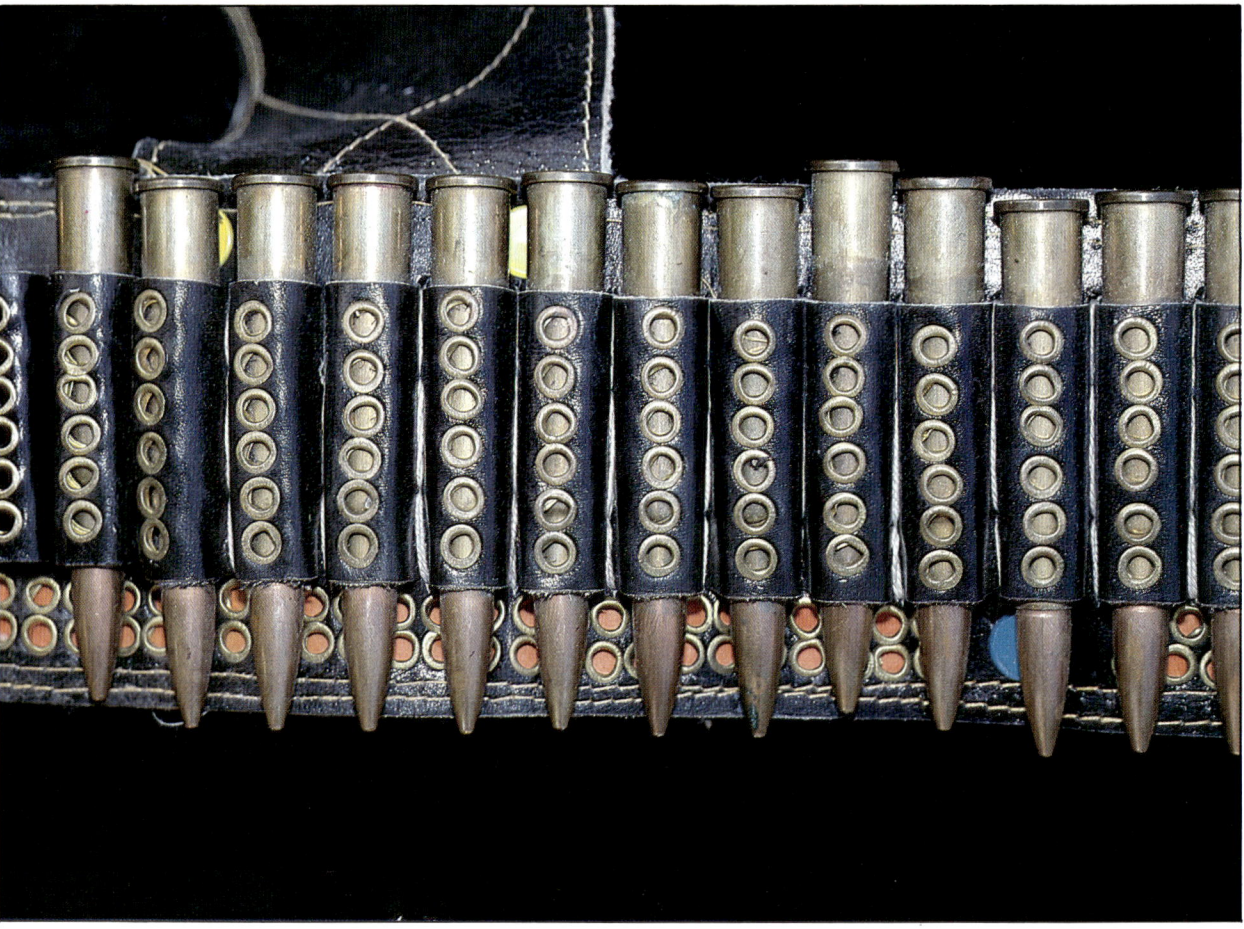

Opposite and below: The Enfield rifle was adapted by Qataris for their use in the desert where it became an essential tool for survival. This finely decorated example, together with gun-belt was owned, as the Arabic inscription declares, by Fahad. (*From the collection at Department of Tourism and Antiquities*: Vine).

Right: A traditional dagger (*Vine*).

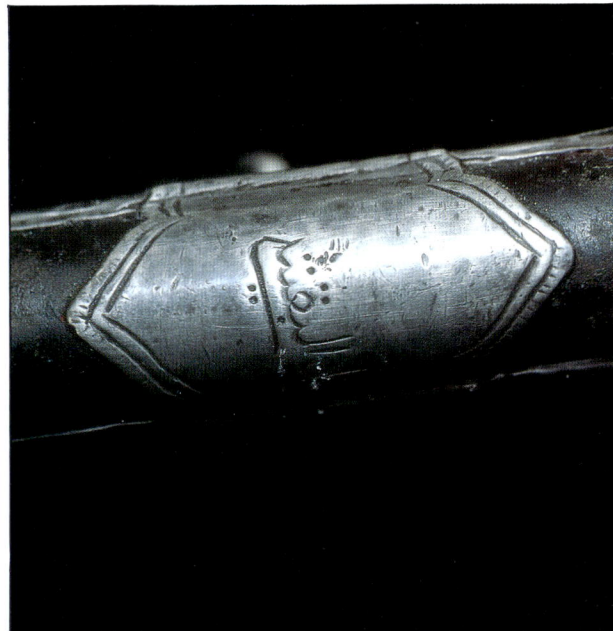

HISTORY AND TRADITIONS

Top left: Traditional shop in the old souk of Doha. (*Ministry of Information and Culture*).

Bottom left: Coffee pot maker. (*Ministry of Information and Culture*).

Opposite and below: Incense or oud burning plays an important part in Arabic hospitality with locally crafted incense burners still in demand. (*Ministry of Information and Culture*).

Ottoman withdrawal from Qatar

When, in 1902, the legendary Ibn Said, grandson of Faisal bin Turki, and a small band of followers recaptured Riyadh, Qasim embraced their austere beliefs and courted Ibn Saud with money and other gifts, despite the displeasure of the Turks: his brother Ahmed, however, did not share his enthusiasm. Captain Prideaux recorded his impressions of Shaikh Qasim when he paid an official visit to Qatar in November of 1905.

"Sheikh Jasim-bin-Thani is a typical patriach of the ancient type, about 80 years of age, with long white beard, and nearly blind from opthalmia, but still vigorous in mind and healthy in body... The Sheikh is still much interested in politics, but he told me that he had retired from all administrative work..."

Qasim's brother Ahmad who managed the day-to-day affairs of the country was murdered by his servant that same year and Abdulla, Qasim's son, took his place. But the venerable old warrior, still in excellent health and in full possession of his

HISTORY AND TRADITIONS

faculties, continued to play a prominent role until his death in 1913, when he was finally succeeded by Abdulla.

1913 also witnessed the further dilution of Ottoman influence in Qatar and the strengthening of Qatari links with the Saudis and the British Government: both these new allegiances were dictated by pragmatic factors. The strong Saudi presence on Qatar's indeterminate desert boundary dictated a friendly relationship with its powerful neighbour and, despite their turbulent relationship with the British Government, the Al Thani were, as we have already seen, eager to use Britain as a means of evicting the Turks. Two months before Qasim's death, al Hasa was recaptured by victorious Saudi forces, ending a lengthy period of domination by the Ottoman Turks. That same year under the unratified Anglo-Turkish Convention, the Ottoman Empire formally renounced all rights to Qatar. Bahrain immediately attempted to enforce the payment of tribute under the terms of the 1868 treaty but Article 10 of the Convention precluded any interference in the internal affairs of Qatar by Bahrain.

The Ottoman entry into World War I on the side of the Central Powers had an enormous impact on the political structures in the Gulf. In 1915 Qatar's last remaining ties with the Turkish Empire were finally divested when they evacuated Doha after 44 years of occupation. Ibn Saud, under the terms of an agreement concluded with Britain in 1915, had pledged to abstain from meddling in the affairs of the states, including Qatar, on the Arabian shores of the Gulf. The way was now clear for Britain to cement its growing influence in Qatar. Up until this time, Qatar was the only place on the western littoral whose pearling fleet was not entitled to protection by British vessels.

Anglo-Qatari treaty of 1916

Under the terms of the 1916 Anglo-Qatar treaty, negotiated with a rather hesitant Abdulla who had no real desire to replace one fetter on Qatar's independence with another, the ruler "placed Qatar on much the same footing as the Trucial shaikhdoms who had signed the same agreement in 1892, for in it, the ruler undertook not to cede, sell, lease or mortgage any of his territory without British consent; not to have relations with

HISTORY AND TRADITIONS

Leather-work on water bags for camel saddles is a local craft under threat from modern synthetics. (*Ministry of Information and Culture*).

any foreign power without British consent; to accept the establishment of post and telegraph offices; to admit British subjects to Qatar and to protect them; to accept the stationing at Doha of a British agent if Britain desired it; and to desist from piracy, the slave trade and arms traffic." However, in recognition of the relatively benign form of slavery practised in this area, which bore no relationship to its colonial counterpart, the ruler and his people were allowed to retain the slaves already in their possession. In fact, most domestic slaves preferred to remain in their secure position as members of their owner's household rather than face the economic uncertainties of the period. As a further concession to entice Abdulla to sign, it was agreed between the negotiating parties that the clauses referring to the British agent, British postal and telegraphic offices, and the protection of British residents, were to remain dormant for the present. In addition, unlike the protection afforded to the other Trucial shaikhdoms, Abdulla persuaded the British to extend their protective umbrella over Qatar both by land and sea. However, although Abdulla believed that the inclusion of the clause XI which read: "They [the British Government] also undertake to grant me good offices, should I or my subjects be assailed by land within the territories of Qatar" was a concrete commitment to active protection, the British Government followed a highly restrictive interpretation stating that "it did not......in practice impose any very serious liability on His Majesty's Government". In reality the British, decidedly reluctant to embroil themselves in the internal affairs of Qatar, persisted in interpreting their treaty relations in the manner best suited to their own ends.

Oil concession and protection agreement: 1935

The defeat of Germany in World War I and the dismantling of the Ottoman Empire with the subsequent institution of British mandates in Iraq and Palestine, accompanied by a strong British presence in Iran, and its control of the local powers through the Trucial system, meant that Britain reigned supreme in the Gulf in 1919. However British supremacy was short-lived as it could not contain the nationalist tendencies prevailing in the Middle East. The rise to power of Riza Khan in Persia in 1921 with a subsequent diminution in British influence also meant that the Arabian shores of the Gulf assumed a new level of importance, not only to the British administration in India, but to the British seat of power in London.

Qatar struggled on through this difficult period at the beginning of the 20th century. The 1930's were particularly arduous since the pearl industry in the Gulf was in crisis due to falling demand in the recession-hit western world and the marketing of a Japanese invention, the cultured pearl. But the 1930's were also to witness the awakening of a new hope for the Gulf which was to radically alter its position on the world stage. Already involved in oil exploration in Persia and Iraq, British officialdom was, at first, extremely sceptical about the oil potential of the Arabian peninsula. It was only when the American-based oil company Socal obtained concessions in Bahrain, after the British-controlled Iraq Petroleum Company (IPC) had turned down the offer, that Britain woke up to the opportunities slipping through their fingers. Socal struck oil in Bahrain in 1932 and also negotiated a concession with Ibn Saud.

The British Government were now determined to confine the further exploration for oil in the area to British companies. Qatar, long rebuffed by Britain, suddenly found itself the focus of attention. The ruler of Qatar, under Article V of the 1916 treaty, had undertaken not to grant a concession without the approval of the British Government. However, details of the attractive terms offered by Socal, terms that had won for it the concession from Ibn Saud, soon reached the shores of the Gulf, making it more difficult for the British to convince Abdulla that his best interests lay with the miserly offerings of the IPC. Indeed Abdulla was unaware of the vast wealth that could be unlocked by oil exploration, partly because the British officials were at pains to disguise this aspect of the deal in case it complicated their negotiations. As a result, however, Abdulla approached the commercial agreement with a view to wringing as much political advantage as possible from the British. Fowle, British Resident in Bushire, negotiating on behalf of the Anglo-Persian Oil Company (APOC), was impatient to complete the deal, particularly since he had been informed by the India Office that the Anglo-Qatari Treaty had been made personal to Abdulla and was not binding to his heirs and successors. But he had to content himself with protracted negotiations until, early in 1935, a formal exchange of letters took place between Fowle and Abdullah before the signing of the commercial agreement.

A mixture of shrewdness, tenacity and political acumen had enabled Abdulla to extract from the British many of the considerations he had been led to believe were originally covered by the 1916 treaty. He was now guaranteed protection by the British government in the event of external "serious and unprovoked attacks"; and his son Hamad was formally recognised as his heir as long as Hamad promised to accept the 1916 treaty on his accession. In order to provide this level of protection, facilities were granted to the RAF in Qatar. The question of jurisdiction over foreigners was also settled to Abdulla's advantage. Following these preliminaries, a document

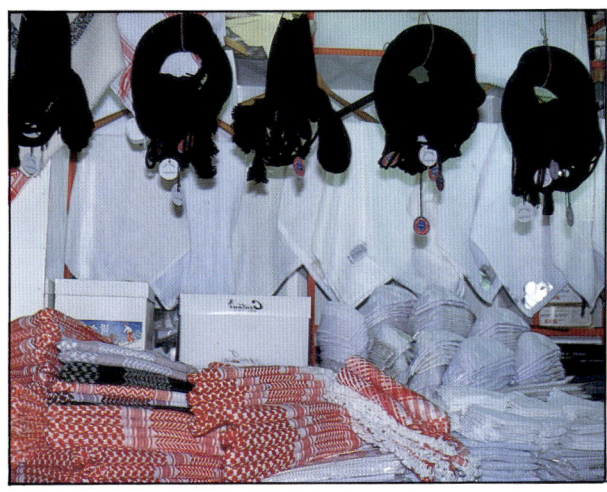

In Doha's traditional material and clothing souk. (*Vine*).

was signed on 17 May 1935 granting APOC, for the next 75 years, the exclusive rights for production, transportation, refining and marketing of petroleum as well as for natural gases and other by-products. In return, after a series of down payments, Abdulla was to be paid royalties of 3 rupees per ton if oil was discovered. A map attached to the concession defined the territory of

HISTORY AND TRADITIONS

Traditional Qatari clothes are charmingly displayed by these young Qataris growing up in a modern society which still honours and respects its customs and traditions. (*Ministry of Information and Culture*).

Qatar. Qatari oil was eventually discovered in October of 1939 but the advent of World War II disrupted the planned production and it wasn't until 1949 that exploitation of the country's oil resources began in earnest.

Boundary agreements

Following the signing of the protection agreement and the granting of the oil concession, the British Government took its responsibilities towards Qatar more seriously. Already a popular and astute leader, Abdulla's position was further bolstered by the protection agreement and especially the acknowledgement of his son and heir. This new security was noticeable in his dealings with Ibn Saud, who, by 1925, controlled vast stretches of the Arabian peninsula. In 1926 Ibn Saud became King of the Hijaz and, in 1932, he was installed as King of Saudi Arabia.

The demarcation of the desert boundaries between Qatar and Saudi Arabia took on new significance with the oil discoveries of the 1930's. Tracts of barren limitless desert, inhabited by a small number of hardy nomads roaming their sandy reaches, now became extremely valuable as possible sources of the black gold that was to change the face of the peninsula. But Ibn Saud, an astute diplomat, indefatigable pragmatist, and a great believer in the value of dialogue, never accepted the "Blue Line" demarcation laid down in the unratified Anglo-Turkish convention of 1913 which was adhered to in the 1935 Agreement, but he continued to discuss the matter with Britain, even after the signing of the Anglo-Qatari agreement. Britain, for its part, valued Saud's continuing friendship in the light of its declining British interests in the Near East. It wasn't until 1965 that an amicable settlement to the thorny subject was attained. In the intervening years the two countries gradually began to appreciate the enormous extent of the petroleum resources and the unprecedented impact these would have on each state's economic and social development. The Saudi-Qatar border dispute was not the only long-standing issue which came

HISTORY AND TRADITIONS

to a head after the signing of the protection agreement with Britain; controversy regarding ownership of Zubara was settled in 1937.

The foundations of a modern administration.
Against the background of the 1935 agreement the Al Thani family continued to guide Qatar's development towards a modern fully-independent state, a process which had its foundation in the mid-nineteenth century. By 1944 Abdulla, now in his eighties but still vigorous and alert, had relinquished much of the day to day management of the shaikhdoms affairs to his son Hamad, who, although he had inherited his father's innate qualities of leadership, deferred to Abdulla's wise judgement in all major decisions. Unfortunately Hamad also suffered from ill-health and often had to rely on his father's help when he was rendered inactive by one of his many ailments. This was a difficult period for Qatar as all oil exploration had been suspended during the war.

The country's work force, already hit by the decline in the pearl industry, was further demoralised when even the jobs generated by the oil company's drilling operations vanished: food was also scarce as a consequence of the war and so the emigration of Qataris continued. Neither Hamad or Abdulla lived to see the benefits of oil production spread throughout the population of Qatar. Hamad died in 1948 and Ali, his eldest brother, became ruler in 1949 when Abdulla abdicated because of old age. Ali's son Ahmad came to power in 1960 on Ali's abdication.

In February of 1972, the present Emir, H.H.Shaikh Khalifa bin Hamad Al Thani, with the support of the ruling family, the Qatari people, and the armed forces, assumed the leadership of a fully-independent Qatar whose protection agreement with Britain had been abandoned in 1970. Even before he became ruler Shaikh Khalifa was responsible for government planning, policy and implementation. Government departments, foundations of the modern administration, were set up in the 1960s in an attempt to marry the old tribal ways with the modern era of technological development. Rapidly increasing oil revenues funded the changes that had to be made although, in contrast to some of its neighbours, Qatar did not have an instant overwhelming oil boom, allowing the burgeoning population a welcome breathing space to make necessary adjustments to their improved circumstances.

HISTORY AND TRADITIONS

FALCONRY

Hassan Sultan Juman Naimi is a reknowned Qatari falconer who has an especially close relationship with his falcon. He can be found on most days at Zubara fort where he is its curator. (*Vine*).

Nasser Jaber Naimi has learnt a great deal about falconry from his family who have practised the art for generations. He regularly hunts the deserts of northern Qatar with his trained falcon. (*Vine*).

NATURAL HISTORY

Natural History

One's initial impression of Qatar is of a low, flat, sand-plain with precious little to relieve the eye. There is, however, a great deal to fascinate the inquisitive naturalist who takes the time to investigate a little further. First of all, Qatar is not entirely flat. Although it's highest point is just 103 metres above sea-level, the effects of even small elevation are emphasised by the generally low-relief of the surrounding countryside. In addition, there are marked regional variations in the form of the landscape, with the most dramatic difference occurring along the southern borders of Qatar where massive sand-dunes rise abruptly from a level desert plain, their sharpened crests and wind-scalloped sides forming an alluring ocean of sand challenging the adventurous traveller to explore each hidden recess. Even the low, flat plains are full of interest for here one may encounter evidence of ancient settlers, not by digging, but right on the surface, where wind, sun and rain have played their part in eroding the substrate, and where stone implements, fragments of ancient pottery, or perhaps the remains left by fishermen, are visible.

It is not just the archaeological record which merits study. There can be few places on earth where a country's geological history is so clearly evidenced by its landscape and rocks. Indeed, geologists have found a great deal to interest them in Qatar and the story they have unravelled bears significance, not just for this over eleven thousand square metres of peninsula, but for the entire Arabian Gulf. Neither is the inquisitive observer confined to collecting fossils and rocks, for a great deal of the wildlife of this desert terrain has survived intact despite the inevitable onslaught on the environment by urban and industrial developments and their attendant infrastructures. Given the climatic conditions and generally salt ridden soils, it is surprising how well many plants do grow and one cannot but admire their adaptive capabilities. Qatar's terrestrial wildlife includes a number of small nocturnal mammals and a range of reptiles together with an interesting array of butterflies and other insects. Then there is the sea, the raison d'etre for many Qatari's to have settled here in the first

Opposite: Typical desert scenery in Qatar (*Vine*).

Right: *Blepharis ciliaris*, locally known as 'Shawk-ul-Dab', is a robust annual herb found in stony and gravelly habitats in Qatar. (*Beniston*).

NATURAL HISTORY

Khor al Udeid, at the south-eastern border Qatar is a shallow inlet from the sea where some of the country's finest beaches and dramatic sand dunes are situated. (*Vine*).

Sand-dunes in Qatar are most abundant in the southern region, especially around Khor Al Udeid, towards the Empty Quarter. (*Ministry of Information and Culture*).

place. Apart from a rich assemblage of edible fish and particularly succulent shrimps, there are vast quantities of the animal upon which the entire economy was once based: the two local species bear the Latin names *Pinctada margaritifera* and *Pinctada radiata* but to the layman they are better known as "pearl-oysters". Finally, there is Qatar's bird-life which is made up, not just of resident birds, but of many regular migratory visitors together with others who fetch-up here, having been blown off route, or perhaps decide to rest at one of the recently created drainage ponds- the result of urban and agricultural developments; these have in fact led to an increase in the numbers of winter visiting birds. Indeed, the "greening of the desert", so much a feature of today's Arabia, has brought about a large increase in the bird population of the entire subcontinent; in many cases turning casual migrants into resident breeders. Thus, to the amateur naturalist, Qatar offers a wide range of interesting wildlife. While some studies have been carried out already there is still much to be done and no doubt a great deal to still be discovered. In this brief over-view we shall look at the current state of knowledge concerning the wildlife of Qatar. We are greatly indebted to members of the Science Faculty at Qatar University who have kindly provided information from their own studies. Individual scientists are separately credited in connection with their own particular contributions.

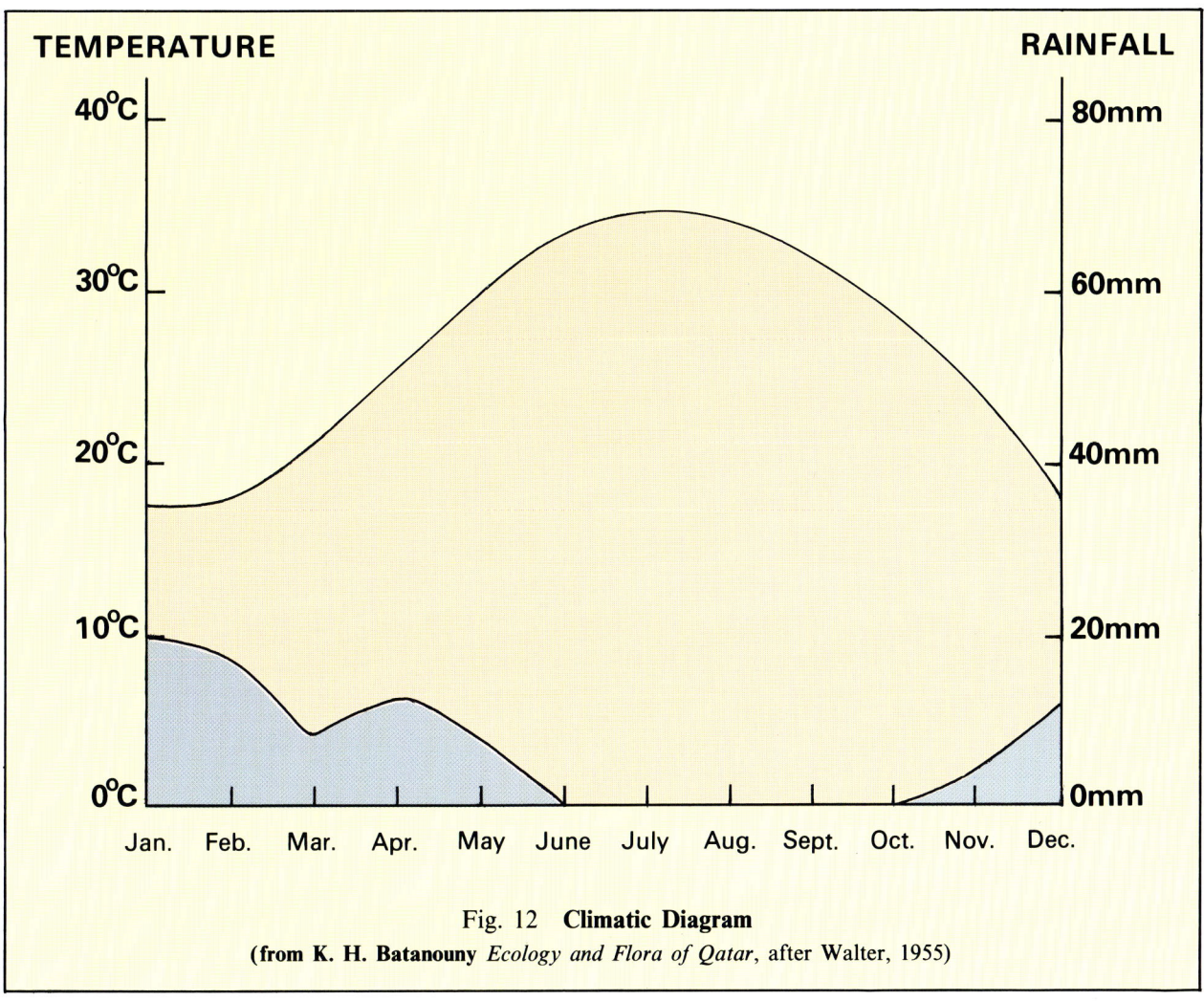

Fig. 12 Climatic Diagram
(from K. H. Batanouny *Ecology and Flora of Qatar*, after Walter, 1955)

Climate

Officially Qatar has a "moderate desert climate", i.e. one in which the seasonal and diurnal temperature extremes of inland desert regions are moderated by the Gulf's sea-breezes. The fact that Qatar is so flat in profile results in low levels of precipitation (5 to 7 cms per year average) and moderate humidity compared to some of the other Gulf countries. When it does rain in Qatar, generally around December-January, rain-showers can be very heavy and are sometimes accompanied by hail. In winter the weather tends to be sunny and quite pleasant in the day with noticeably cooler nights. The January temperature range thus fluctuates between a daily maximum of around 25°C with a minimum night temperature of 7°C This contrasts sharply with the almost unbearable heat of mid-summer when nights are only just cool enough, at around 22°C to bring much relief from the searing daytime heat which can go as high as 46°C Even at this time, however, northerly winds tend to moderate the air temperature and in the process lower humidity levels.

Table 2. Average monthly temperature and humidity rates at Doha International Airport.

	Temperature Deg. Celsius		Humidity (%)	
	Max.	Min.	0600hrs	1800hrs
January	25.5	7.4	78	81
February	30.3	9.5	72	76
March	33.2	9.6	54	67
April	39.6	14.4	32	67
May	43.8	19.0	32	52
June	46.7	22.3	37	42
July	45.3	24.9	41	63
August	45.1	24.5	49	66
September	43.7	21.4	57	70
October	39.3	18.7	58	71
November	34.6	13.5	64	69
December	27.6	9.0	68	74

Geology

The most obvious feature of Qatar's geological past is that the entire surface land-mass is dominated by sedimentary rocks originating beneath the shallow waters of the Arabian Gulf. In order to appreciate the processes and sequences involved, one must first look at the evidence for sea-level fluctuations. The extensive consolidated dune deposits, or aeolianites, at various sites such as bays along the eastern side of Ras Abaruk peninsula and at "hills" like Jebel Jusasiyah, Jebel Wakrah and those at al-Wusail, all tell a tale of a once more exposed foreshore, providing the wind-blown sand from which the dunes were formed. Radiocarbon dating of fossiliferous remains has helped to provide a picture of sea-level chronology. While more work remains to be done, the picture now emerging shows that the shallow depression of the Arabian Gulf was all above sea-level between about 70,000 and 44,000 years ago. Despite the absence of an archaeological record Man must have roamed across the entire land, between what is today Arabia and Iran, searching for game and gathering seeds or fruit. Probably during summer-time the inhabitants migrated towards higher land whilst in winter they may well have descended and ranged out over this vast swampy delta. Between 44,000 and around 30,000 years ago the sea encroached gradually into the Gulf and brought with it marine-life which would no doubt have been harvested from time to time, presumably at low-tide. The sea once more receded and by 15,000 years ago the entire Gulf was once again dry. When the shallow sand-flats dried out they of course provided the material which winds whipped into tall undulating dunes. These were formed across the present sea-bed of the Gulf, as well as along today's coastal fringes and further inland. In addition to the marine sands however, terrigenous materials were carried across the depression by flash-floods. Soils deposited in this manner on the bed of the Gulf no doubt provided a substrate for various plants and in turn for grazing animals. Qatar thus gained a patchily distributed thin topsoil and irregular outcrops of vegetation. When the sea made its final (or most recent) incursion, back into the Gulf, it once more brought a rich assemblage of marine-life complementing the somewhat meagre terrestrial resources. Taken together, Qatar's land and coastal waters subsequently provided a suitable place for Man to settle. The exploitability of the coast was however reduced by development of sabkhas, a process promoted by coastal uplift and a decelerating rise in sea-level. Much more recently, during the Islamic period, silts accumulated at certain sites, such as Umm al Salal, rendering them attractive for permanent settlements to be established.

The rise and fall of mean sea-level in the Gulf was thus a major influence in establishing the

Left: Limestone outcrops near Dukhan showing wind-erosion. (*Vine*).

sedimentary layers and providing materials for soil formation while also greatly affecting the suitability of Qatar as a place for Man to live. In fact, when we look closely at the environmental history of the area, there are only two periods which appear to have been suitable for Man to establish settlements on Qatar. These are around 6,000 years ago, and during the last 1,500 or so years. At other times Man most probably utilised the land in a very temporary manner rather than establishing permanent bases there. This picture corresponds well with the archaeological record outlined in chapter one. Sea levels have still not stabilised and evidence from the last eight thousand years indicates fluctuations of up to two metres in mean sea-level with high tide reaching about two metres above today's levels during the period four to seven thousand years ago. Following that the sea receded until it reached today's level at some time between three and four thousand years ago. Then, in the second half of the second millenium, it rose once more, probably reaching +1.0 m. before dropping again. Biological evidence of such sea-level movements includes radiocarbon dating of *Cerithium* shells collected from a shale outcrop corresponding to a sea-level of +2.0m: the fossils were dated to around 3,380 to 4,670 years B.P. One other consequence of Qatar's submersion and gradual emersion is that evaporation of seawater in the sediment has left behind a variety of salt deposits, including a large amount of gypsum. Associated with these gypsum deposits are characteristic "desert roses" which may be found quite commonly in the sabkha close to the industrial NGL complex at Umm Said. A particularly common crystalline form, in sabkha around the outskirts of Umm Said, is that of twinned gypsum crystals, about two centimetres long, and a shape reminiscent of a swallow's tail. These are formed as winter high-tides flood the mud-flats, trapping seawater in shallow depressions where summer heat causes rapid evaporation and crystalline formation. In order to find the desert roses close to the Umm Said NGL plant it is necessary to actually dig into the sand to a depth of about a metre, just above the water table. Interestingly enough, gypsum has played a vital role in creation of the great oil and natural gas resources of the Arabian Gulf. Gypsum, deposited in a similar fashion to that which we can witness today, but

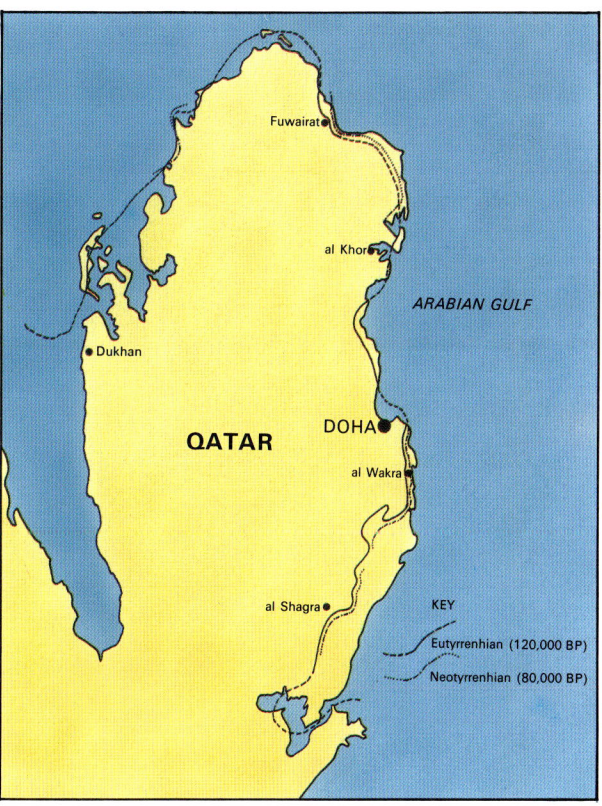

Fig. 13 **Pleistocene shorelines of Qatar Peninsula**
(from Ministry of Information *Mission Archaeologique Française à Qatar*, Tome 1, after J. P. Perthuisot, 1977b)

Fig. 14 **Flandrian coastal formations of Qatar peninsula—6000 BP**
(from Ministry of Information *Mission Archaeologique Française à Qatar*, Tome 1, after J. P. Perthuisot, 1977b)

Fig. 15 **Variations of shorelines since 6000 BP in Khor al Udeid area** (from Ministry of Information *Mission Archaeologique Française à Qatar*, Tome 1, after J. P. Pertuisot and A. Jausein, 1978)
A. Location
B. Maximum Flandrian transgression
C. Assumed intermediate situation
D. Present coastline

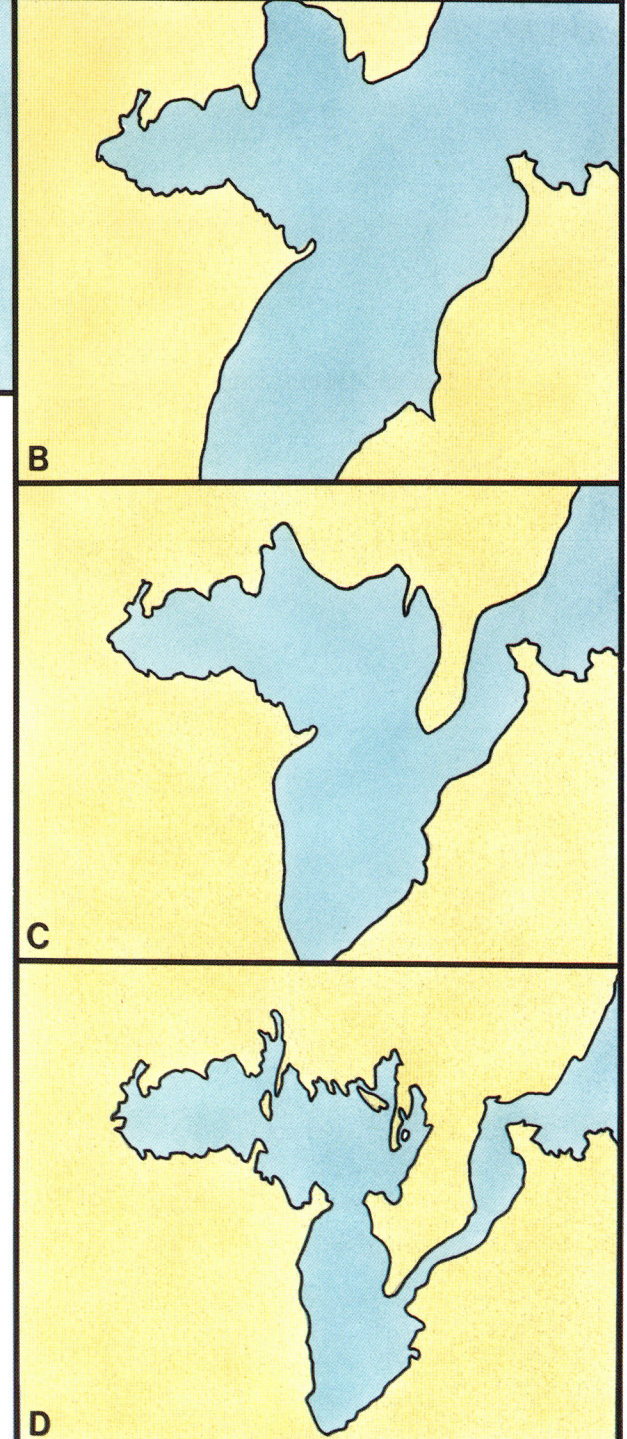

laid down between 140 and 190 million years ago, in the Jurassic period, has since recrystallised to form a dense impervious capping of anhydrite overlying porous limestones and dolomites in which the hydrocarbons are held.

What of Qatar's earlier geology? One form of evidence which has attracted the attention of both amateur and professional geologists is that of fossiliferous sharks' teeth. In Qatar these may be found loose on the surface or else embedded in a yellowish green shale ("Midra shale") which occurs especially at several sites in the west of the peninsula, together with some isolated outcrops in the east. The shale has been dated to around fifty million years ago so any fossils found within it are of similar age; quite old, one might say, until we realise that sharks are known to have lived for at least four hundred million years! The main point gleaned from such fossils is that at this period the land area we now call Qatar lay beneath the waves, forming a shallow tropical sea-bed over which all forms of sea-life passed. This biologically rich Eocene sea covered the entire peninsula of Qatar which remained underwater until a period of land uplift at the beginning of the Miocene period (about 24 million years ago) brought sections of land above sea-level, and created conditions for consolidation of marine sediments into limestone. This too was a period of rich marine-life whose remains are today preserved as numerous fossil shells and fish bones. Approximately five million years ago a blanket of gravel was washed over much of Qatar, carried by a river flowing from the eastern landmass of Arabia.

The oldest rocks visible on the land surface of Qatar are limestones with heavy salt deposits from the "Rus" formation dating from the lower Eocene, around 55 million years ago. These are present in the centre of Qatar, north-west of Doha; in the core of the eroded Dukhan anticline along the west coast; and along the southern border. In other areas these ancient limestones are covered by more recent rocks. Salts within the "Rus" limestones have been precipitated by evaporation as gypsum and anhydrite (i.e. calcium sulphate), and as rock-salt or halite. Both these salts are easily dissolved and, where ground water is present, the dissolution of salts within "Rus" limestone has caused the rock to break down leaving large depressions. This has occurred particularly in the south of Qatar, causing rain-water to be lost from the surface layers.

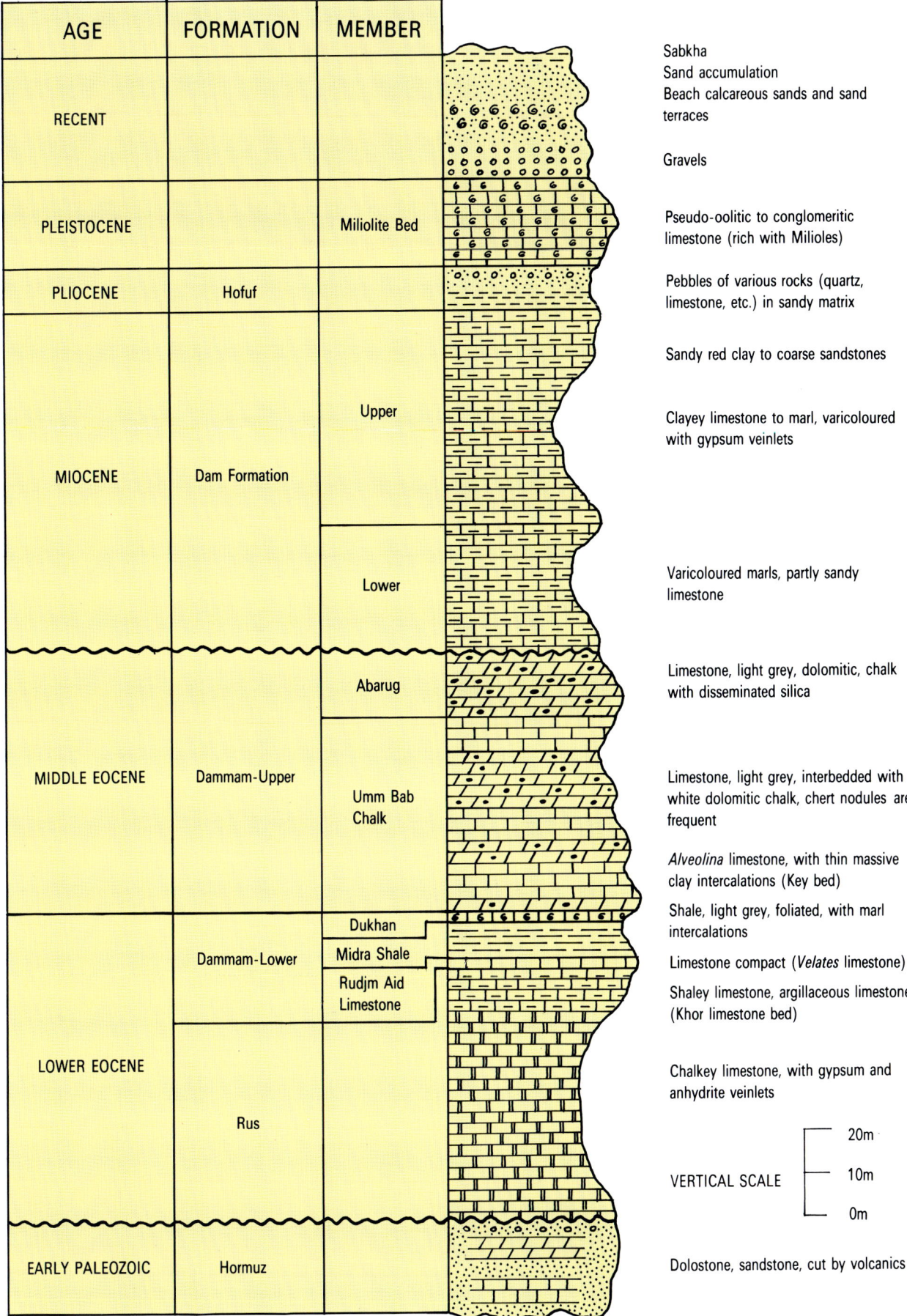

Fig.16 **Composite columnar setting representing the rock sequence in Qatar.**
(after K. H. Batanouny *Ecology and Flora of Qatar*, 1981)

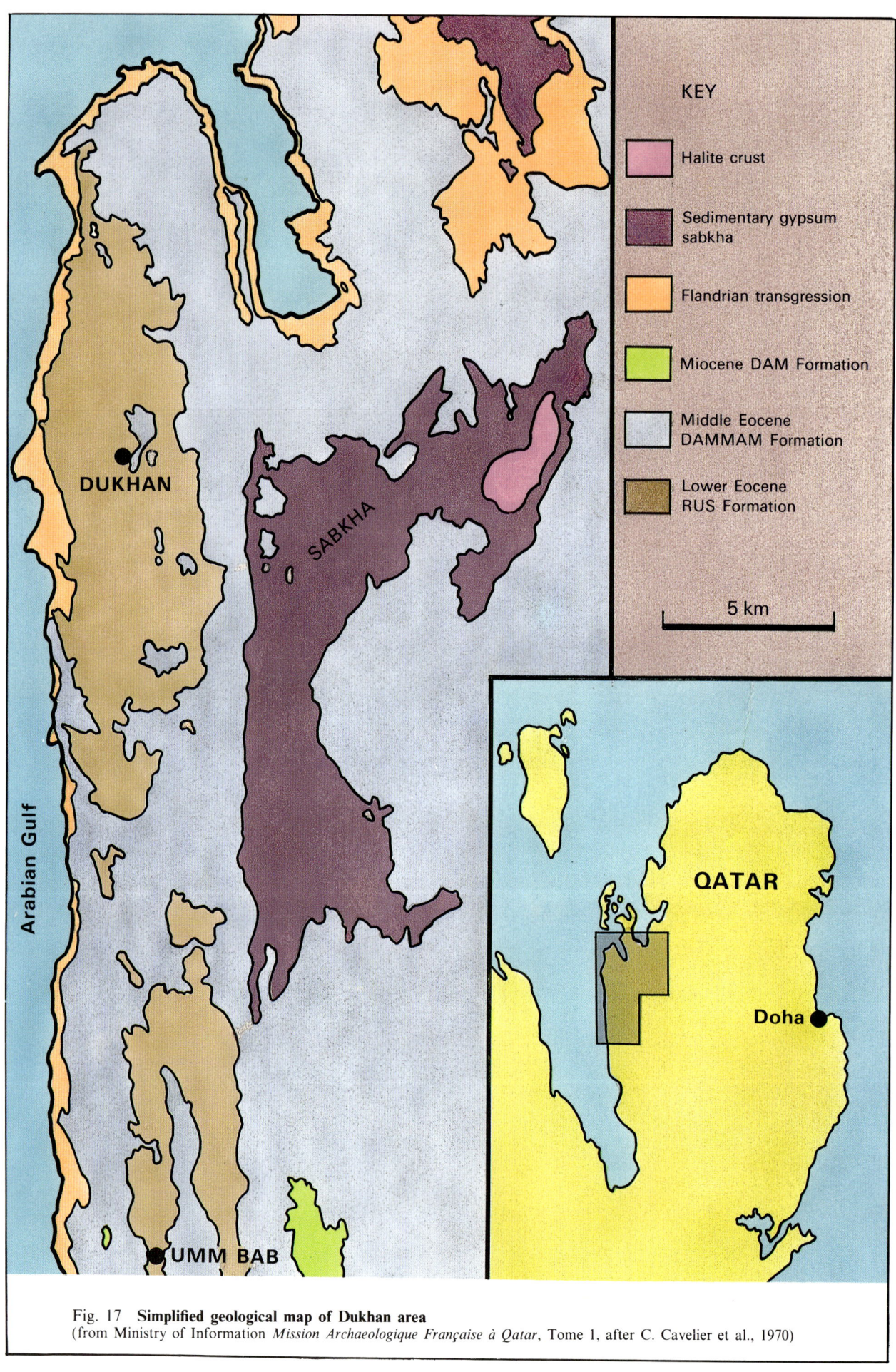

Fig. 17 **Simplified geological map of Dukhan area**
(from Ministry of Information *Mission Archaeologique Française à Qatar*, Tome 1, after C. Cavelier et al., 1970)

Date palms flourish in Qatar's oases, providing a traditional ingredient to the local diet. (*Vine*).

Rocks overlying the "Rus" were laid down later in the Eocene when marine-life flourished in the shallow waters which covered Qatar and surrounding areas, forming a blanket of fine silt and mud rich in fossils, known to geologists as the "Damman formation". It is at the base of this layer, in the "Midra shale", that amateur naturalists take delight in seeking fossil sharks' teeth mentioned above. It outcrops along the inner edge of the Dukhan anticline, a favourite hunting ground for fossil hunters.

Another interesting geological formation are "Mesas", box-like hills arising abruptly from the stony desert, creating a distinctive feature of the southern region of Qatar. The limestones and clays from which these mesas are formed are full of fossil shells, corals, echinoderms, crabs and reptilian bones. They were laid down during the Miocene and are largely concealed today by a thin covering of sand and gravel known as the "Hofuf formation".

Physical geography

Qatar is an eleven thousand four hundred and thirty seven square kilometre, low-lying peninsula protruding from the main land-mass of eastern Arabia into the shallow Gulf. Its north-south axis stretches for about 180 kms, while its greatest width along the east-west axis is about 85 kms. In addition to the peninsula itself Qatar has some small off-lying islands. Early maps of the region tended to greatly under-estimate the size of Qatar, or else to assume that it was an island rather than an appendage of the mainland. The first detailed survey was in 1825 when the Indian Naval vessels "Discovery" and "Psyche" undertook a survey of the western coastline of the Gulf, but even they skipped some sections in the Bay of Salwa. Arabian interest in Qatar focussed initially upon its extensive pearl beds and later as a haven for trading vessels. European knowledge of the interior of Qatar is relatively recent, Herman Burchardt's 1904 excursion from Salwa to Doha providing the first recorded investigation of the inland areas.

The physical geography of Qatar has been greatly affected by Man's activities, particularly since the discovery of oil. Today the main town of Doha is a burgeoning modern city while vast desert areas are now irrigated by waste-water and criss-crossed by pipe-lines transporting oil from producing fields at Dukhan to huge refineries or to crude oil termini at Umm Said. Previous shortages of fresh-water have been largely reversed through desalination plants utilising sea-water and enabling cultivation of areas previously considered impossible to farm. Road construction has resulted in easy access to most regions of the country while four-wheel drive vehicles have opened up desert regions where previously Man was dependent upon walking or riding camels.

As we have seen above, Qatar is comprised mainly of surface Eocene limestone and gypsum which is overlain towards the south by Miocene marls and limestone. The generally low relief is broken by a 35 mile long, gentle anticline reaching almost 62 metres, upon which is situated Qatar's major oil-field. A second rise occurs towards the mid-line of the peninsula, while mention has been made of the conspicuous mesas in the west and sand-dunes of the south where the highest elevation is 103m above sea-level. The land area of Qatar may be conveniently separated into three main areas; the limestone plateau; the sandy southern region; and the coastline with extensive sabkhas.

NATURAL HISTORY

Clockwise, from top left:

Glossonema edule is a common plant in Qatar where it is known as 'Itr' while the edible fruits are called 'Garawah'. (*Beniston*).

Senecio sp., locally known as 'Zimloog', is a relatively rare plant in Qatar but has benefited from increased irrigation in association with agriculture. (*Beniston*).

Lichen encrusted rocks at Jussasiyah. (*Vine*).

Alhagi maurorum, locally known as 'A'qool', is interesting for its use in traditional local medicine. It is eaten by camels and may be referred to as 'camel-thorn'. (*Beniston*)

Dipcadi erythreum, locally known as 'Mesilmo', is a common bulbous herb in Qatar, growing on sandy and loamy soils, especially in depressions. (*Beniston*).

Plants

By far the most conspicuous plant in Qatar is the ubiquitous Acacia or Samr (*Acacia tortilis*), an exceptionally adaptable, salt tolerant tree whose minute leaves minimise water loss through transpiration, and whose needle sharp spines discourage grazing animals. Qatar's flora has been well described by the Egyptian botanist, Dr Kamaleldin Batanouny, who spent many years studying the country's plants and their ecology. More recently Dr Gamal El-Ghazaly and Mohamed Abdel-eRazik of the University of Qatar have investigated the distribution of plants in Qatar while amateur botanists William and Nicole Beniston have made a survey of the wild flowering plants of the peninsula. The unique characteristics of many desert plants have drawn the attention of biochemists whose interests lie in the chemical structures of different plants. Considerable work in this field of phytochemistry has been carried out by Dr Abdel Fatah Rizq at the University of Qatar. Work on the medicinal properties of various herbs and wild plants in the region has been undertaken by Dr Batanouny. Batanouny describes 301 species belonging to 207 genera and 55 families. In so doing he laid down a challenge to amateur and professional botanists alike, to add to the list and thus increase our knowledge of plant ecology on this generally arid peninsula.

A large area of Qatar is taken up by slightly elevated stony or gravelly land described as "hamada" and known locally as "hazm" or "mistah". While relatively little grows here the characteristic plants such as *Zygophyllum*

Cistanche phelypaea, locally called 'Dhanoun', is a root parasite, especially growing on *Limonium axillare* and *Arthrocnemum glaucum* on coastal saline flats in Qatar. (*Beniston*).

Aizoon canariensis is locally known as Gafnah. It is very common in Qatar especially in shallow depressions and along roadsides. (*Beniston*).

Left: *Abutilon fruticosa* is often found growing in association with *Ziziphus* bushes which provide some protection for this shrub. (*Beniston*).

Opposite: *Ziziphus nummularia*, locally known as 'Sidr', grows in 'roda' or slight depressions where ground water accumulates in central Qatar. Typically, accumulations of fine sand build up around the base of the tree. Three pictures indicate (a) general view of terrain in which they are growing; (b) close view of single tree, (c) close-up of vegetation of same tree. (*Vine*).

quatarense, *Acacia tortilis*, and *Lycium shawii* are quite conspicuous. Here and there across the land-scape, broad shallow depressions referred to locally as "rodat" occur, probably as a result of sub-surface solution of evaporites. As centres for accumulation of rainwater run-off, these have much richer assemblages of plant species than the hamada with variations in dominance dependent primarily upon the substrate grain size. Once again, *Lycium shawii* (known as "*Awsaj*") is widespread, whilst *Ziziphus nummularia* favours deep fine textured, water transported deposits. Where soils are shallower, but still water-borne, the grass *Cymbopogon parkeri* flourishes in spring. *Acacia tortilis*, favours depressions with shallow surface deposits and occasionally outcropping bedrocks while *Acacia ehrenbergiana* dominates in finer, compact, silty soils. Wind-blown sandy depressions towards the south of Qatar are dominated by the grass *Panicum turgidum* (or "*thumam*"), which grows to a metre or more in height, with *Acacia tortilis* inhabiting dryer soil around their perimeters. Depressions with a sediment of fine, water-deposited sand, are frequently inhabited by *Acacia ehrenbergiana* and *Pennisetum divisum*.

While true "wadis" do not occur in Qatar, there are regions in the south where flood waters are channelled through narrow courses or runnels, providing useful habitats for plants such as *Pennisetum divisum*, *Acacia ehrenbergiana*, and *Lycium shawii*. "Markh", or *Leptadenia pyrotechnica* may also be present where sediments are wind-blown.

Sabkhas, i.e. inland or coastal salt-flats, form an important element in Qatar's landscape, accounting for around six percent of the total area. Halophytic plants found here include coastal stands of the mangrove *Avicennia marina* which is especially prevalent opposite Dhahkira, an area proposed as a national nature reserve. Other salt-flat species comprise *Arthrocnemum glaucum*, *Juncus rigidus* and *Aeluropus lagopoides*, *Halocnemum strobiolaceum*, *Halopeplis perfoliata*, *Limonium axillare Sporobolus arabicus*, *Cressa cretica*, *Suaeda vermiculata*, *Halopyrum mucronatum* and the root parasitic Desert Hyacinth, *Cistanche phelypaea*, living in association with *Limonium axillare* and *Arthrocnemum glaucum*.

A preliminary investigation of plant distribution in both hammada and sabkhas within Qatar has been carried out by Gamal El-Ghazaly and Mohamed Abdel-Razik of the University of Qatar, and I am indebted to them for permission to reproduce their findings in figures 18 and 19.

The study of Qatar's plant-life is of more than taxonomic and ecological interest since many of the locally occurring species have been used as constituents in traditional medicines. Today scientists are increasingly aware that biochemical evidence supports many of these natural medicines. Bedu tribesmen have long been aware of the purgative uses of *Citrullus colocynthis* (a member of the water-melon family) or of the pain healing properties of *Teucrium polium* (mint family). Many other plants have properties which enable their use as curatives and research into biochemistry of Qatar's plant-life remains an active field of study among scientists at Qatar University.

NATURAL HISTORY

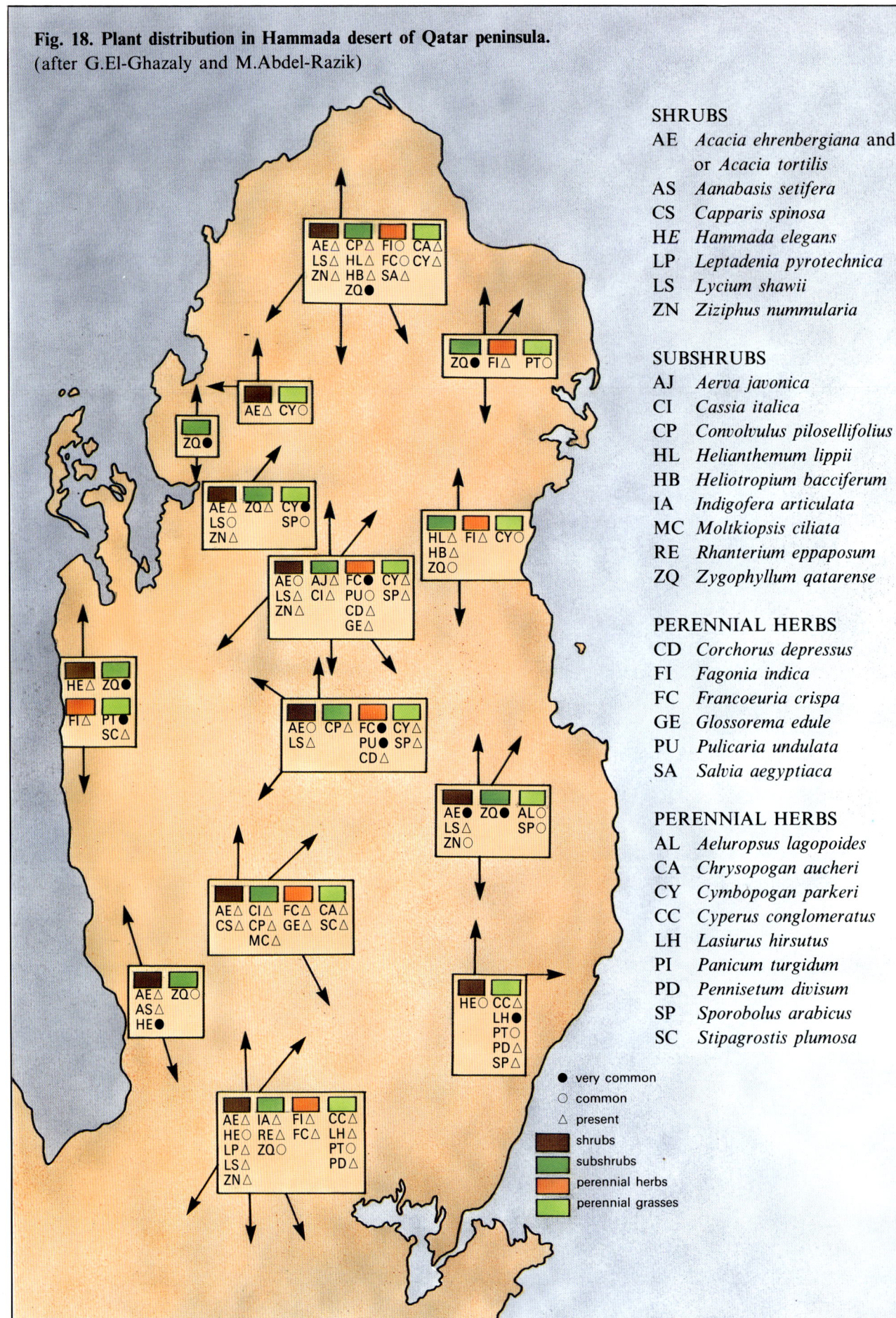

Fig. 18. Plant distribution in Hammada desert of Qatar peninsula. (after G. El-Ghazaly and M. Abdel-Razik)

Early morning dew on *Cyperus conglomeratus* rush seedling at Jussasiyah. (*Vine*).

Lycium shawii, the desert thorn bush. (*Beniston*).

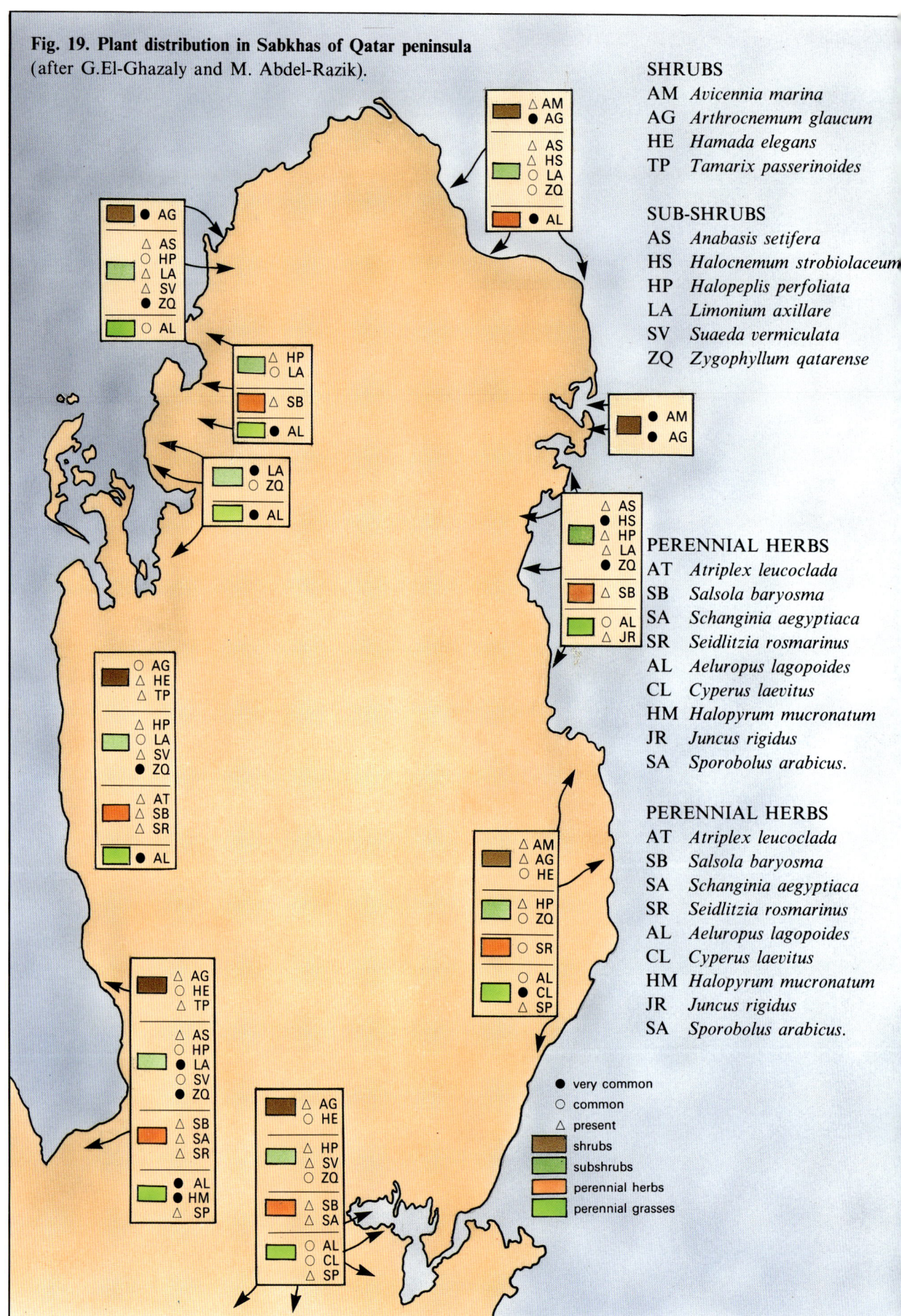

Fig. 19. Plant distribution in Sabkhas of Qatar peninsula (after G. El-Ghazaly and M. Abdel-Razik).

NATURAL HISTORY

Above: *Zygophyllum qatarense*, locally known as 'Harm', owes its specific name to its type locality. It grows in rocky habitats such as that seen here at Jussasiyah. (*Vine*).

Left: *Limonium axillare*, locally known as 'Qataf', is a common halophyte along the coast and saline flats of Qatar. (*Beniston*).

Below: *Halopeplis perfoliata* occurs in coastal salt marsh communities where it may be the dominant plant. (*Vine*).

83

NATURAL HISTORY

Adult and larval stages of Ant Lion and Scarab Beetle

Insects

The insect fauna of Qatar has been investigated by Dr R.M. Abdu of the University of Qatar. His findings are summarised in table 3. The list reveals the presence of plant pests, parasites, and predators together with desertic insects.

Top left and bottom: The honeycomb or nest of wild bees in the garden of Qatar University. (*R. M. Abdu*). Top right: Dr R. M. Abdu during his entomological trip.

Table 3. Insect Fauna of Qatar

(after: R.M.Abdu and N.F.Shaumar, 1985. A Preliminary List of the Insect Fauna of Qatar. Qatar University Science Bulletin. 5: 215-232.)

Order Thysanura
Thermobia domestica

Order Ephemeroptera
Caenis sp.

Order Odonata
Ischnura evansi
Anax parthenope
Diplacodes lefebvrei
Orthetrum sabina
Pantala flavescens
Trithemis annulata

Order Orthoptera
Acrida pellucida
Aiolopus thalassinus
Anacridium aegyptium
Chrotogonus homalodemus
Cyclopternacris etbaica
Leptocyrtus sp.
Locusta danica
Pyrgomorpha cognata
Schistocerca gregarcia
Sphingonotus azurescens
Sphingonotus carinatus
Thisoicetrus littroralis
Thmetis pulchripennis
Truxalis nasuta
Acheta domesticus
Liogryllus bimaculatus
Oecanthus sp.
Gryllotalpa africana
Gryllotalpa gryllotalpa
Conocephalus conocephalus
Homorocryphus nitidulus
Phaneroptera roseata

Order Dictyoptera
Blatella arundinicola
Blatella germanica
Periplaneta americana
Periplaneta tartara
Blepharopsis mendica
Empusa pennata
Fremiaphila spp.
Mantis religiosa
Sphodromantis viridis

Order Isoptera
Anacanthotermes ochraceus
Psammotermes hybostoma

Order Dermaptera
Anisolabis annulipes
Labidura riparia
Labidura confusa

Order Hemiptera
Agraphopus lethierryi
Amphibolus venator
Camptopus lateralis
Cletus sp.
Liorhyssus hyalinus
Nariscus cinctiventris
Sigara sp.
Cydnus hispidulus
Cydnus macrophthalmus
Creontiades pallidus
Dieuches mucronatus
Nysius gramicola
Chroantha orunatula
Eusarcoris inconpicuus
Nezara viridula
Schizops aegyptiaca
Sciocoris conspurcatus
Piezodorus teretipes
Scantius aegyptius
Holotrichius sp.
Reduvius pallipes

Order Neuroptera
Chrysoperla carnea
Anisochrysa amseli
Creoleon klugi
Morter hyalinus

Order Lepidoptera
Papilio demoleus demoleus
Pieris rapae
Pontia glauconome
Anaphaeis aurota aurota
Colias croceus
Madais fausta fausta
Tarucus balkanicus
Tarucus rosaceus
Zizeeria knysna
Lampides boeticus
Danaus chrysippus
   chrysippus
Vanessa cardui
Scopula coenosaria
Scopula ochroleucaria
Autographa gamma
Cornutiplusia circumflexa

Trichoplusia sp.
Utetheisa pulchella
Agrotis ipsilon
Agrotis puta
Clytie haifae
Heliothis peltigera
Heliothis zea
Spodoptera exigua
Spodoptera littoralis
Tathorhynchus exicçota
Echromius ocellae
Cornifrons ulceratalis
Herpetogramma licarsisalis
Nomophila noctuella
Acherontia atropos
Agrius convolvuli
Daphnis nerii
Hippotion celerio
Hyles lineata

Order Coleoptera
Anthia duodecimguttata
Calosoma chlorostictum
Calosoma imbricatum
Cicindela melancholica
Eretes sticticus
Pentodon bispinosus
Phyllogantus cristatus
Scarabaeus sacer
Stalagmopygus albella
Coccinella undecimpunctata
Adesmia spp.
Mesostena angustata
Mesostena elegans
Gonocephalum rusticum
Gonocephalum setulosum
Micipsa sp.
Ocnera philistina
Ocnera hispida
Opatroides punctulatus
Zophosis sp.
Tribolium confusum
Necrobia rufipes
Apomecyna lameerei
Psiloptera mimosae
Lasidoerma serricorne
Oryzaephilus surinamensis

Order Diptera
Culex molestus
Theobaldia sp.
Apoclea algira

Syrphus corollae
Eristalis quinquelineatus
Nemestrinus rufipes
Musca domestica
Musca sorbens
Musca albina
Limnophora notabilis
Limnophora rufimana
Stomoxys calcitrans
Calliphora vicina
Chrysomyia albiceps
Chrysomyia marginals
Lucilia cuprina
Lucilia sericata
Sarcophaga carnaria
Sarcophaga hirtipes
Sarcophaga haemorrhoidalis
Wohlfahrtia indigena
Wohlfahrtia nuba

Order Hymenoptera
Apis fasciata
Apis mellifera
Anthophora klugi
Anthophora albigena
Colletes nanus
Xylocopa aestuans
Xylocopa hottentota
Megachile sp.
Ammophila erminea
Ammophila tydei
Eumenes campaniformis
Liris haemorrhoidalis
Notogonidea nigrita
Notogonidea memnonia
Sceliphron sp.
Sphex niveatus
Sphex albisectus
Cryptochilus discolor
Hexachrysis sp.
Stilbum sp.
Evania appendigaster
Diplazon laetatorius
Barylypa rufa
Ophion sp.
Enicospilus sp.
Brachymeria sp.
Bracon fastidiator
Dielis thoracicus collaris
Camponotus maculatus
   aegyptiacus
Camponotus arenarius

NATURAL HISTORY

Clockwise, from top left: Ant lion pit in sandy soil is about 20-30mm in diameter; the pitted beetle, *Adesmia cancellata*, is commonly found in Qatar wherever there is vegetation; aphids or plant lice, found on all types of plant life; larval stage of the common citrus butterfly, *Papilio demoleus*; large brown cicada, *Cryptotympana mimica*, in the nest position on a tree stem. (*R. M. Abdu*).

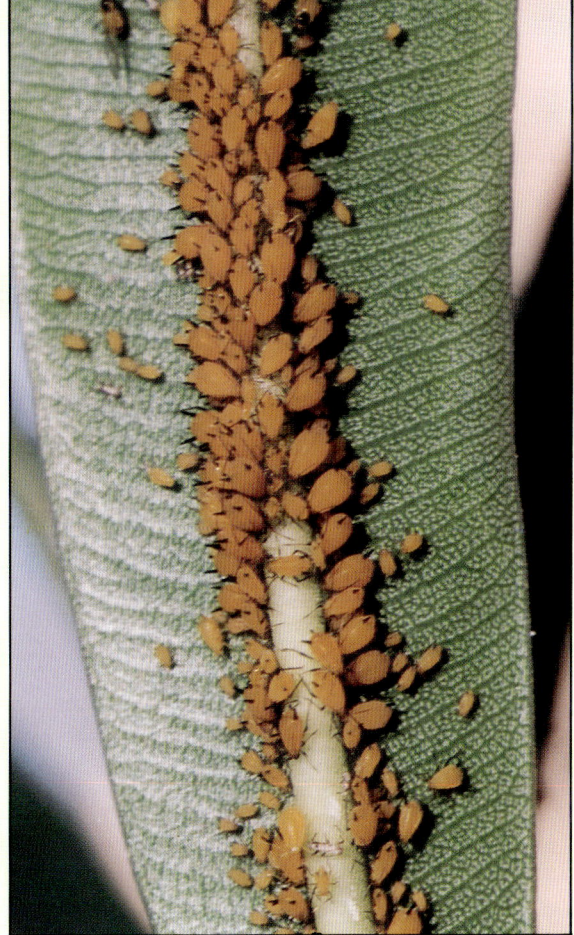

NATURAL HISTORY

This page, top and bottom right: The common citrus butterfly, *Papilio demoleus*.

Centre: *Madais faustra*.

Bottom left: *Vanessa cardui*.

Opposite, top left: *Crocothemis erythraea* has widespread distribution with a preferred habitat of rocky water courses, desert pools and barren irrigation channels.

Bottom: Large brown cicada, *Cryptotympana mimica*, one of the most common species which is found in large numbers throughout all wooded parts of the colony and it occurs seasonally in May, June and July. (R. M. Abdu).

NATURAL HISTORY

Birds

Home to a variety of desert, rural, garden, urban, coastal and sea-birds, Qatar also forms an important resting location for a number of species during autumn and spring migrations. Bird-life encountered depends upon both habitat and season with favoured observation sites along the shore-line; in areas of undisturbed desert; around effluent drainage ponds; and in gardens. While autumn and spring are probably the most rewarding times to study bird-life, there is always something to see and birdwatching remains a most enjoyable pursuit, encouraging excursions to areas of desert or coastline which one might not otherwise visit. Coastal birds such as various gulls, terns, turnstones, sanderlings, kentish plovers, herons and socotra cormorants may be seen throughout the year along much of the shore-line. Visitors to the desert during summer will be unlikely to miss seeing several species of larks including hoopoe, crested and black-crowned finch larks. During the autumn migration the species list grows rapidly with the arrival of swallows, swifts, house martins, a number of warblers, redstarts, shrikes, flycatchers, wheatears, wagtails and falcons including kestrels and harriers. Wintering species include several waders and gulls together with coots and little grebes which remain close to the effluent ponds. During the spring migration birds which passed through in autumn return, on their way north again.

NATURAL HISTORY

Table 4. List Of Qatar's Birds

The following list of Qatar's birds was compiled by Mrs F.E.Warr and first published in the Journal of the Qatar Natural History Group (1983–86 report). At the time of writing an Atlas of Arabian birds is being compiled by Michael Jennings, author of *Birds of the Arabian Gulf* (George Allen & Unwin, 1981). Michael also edits "Phoenix", a newsletter keeping bird-watchers in touch with each other throughout the Middle East. Ornithological records from Qatar (which impinges on eight squares within the Atlas grid) are always welcome and may be sent direct to him (Moonraker Cottage, 1, Eastcourt, Burbage, Marlborough, Wiltshire, SN8 3AG, UK).

Species		Status
Latin Name	**Common Name**	
Struthio caaelus	Ostrich	Extinct
Tachybaptus ruficollis	Little Grebe	RB
Podiceps cristatus	Great Crested Grebe	WV
Podiceps nigricollis	Black-necked Grebe	WV, CB
Puffinus lherminieri	Audubon's Shearwater	Rare, WV
Phaethon aethereus	Red-billed Tropicbird	Rare
Phalacrocorax carbo	Great Cormorant	WV
Phalacrocorax nigrogularis	Socotra Cormorant	RB
Pelecanus onocrotalus	White Pelican	Rare, WV
Botaurus stellaris	Bittern	Rare, WV
Ixobrychus minutus	Little Bittern	PM
Nycticorax nycticorax	Night Heron	PM, WV
Ardeola ralloides	Squacco Heron	PM
Bubulcus ibis	Cattle Egret	PM
Egretta gularis	Western Reef Heron	PM, RB
Egretta garzetta	Little Egret	PM, WV
Egretta alba	Great White Egret	PM, WV
Ardea cinerea	Grey Heron	PM, WV
Ardea purpurea	Purple Heron	PM, WV
Ciconia nigra	Black Stork	Vagrant
Ciconia ciconia	White Stork	Rare, PM
Plegadis falcinellus	Glossy Ibis	PM
Platalea leucorodia	Spoonbill	WV
Phoenicopterus ruber	Greater Flamingo	WV
Anser anser	Greylag Goose	Scarce, WV
Tadorna ferruginea	Ruddy Shelduck	Scarce, WV
Tadorna tadorna	Shelduck	Scarce, WV
Anas penelope	Wigeon	WV
Anas strepera	Gadwall	Scarce, WV
Anas crecca	Teal	PM, WV
Anas platyrhynchos	Mallard	WV
Anas acuta	Pintail	WV
Anas querquedula	Garganey	PM
Anas clypeata	Shoveler	WV
Marmaronetta angustirostris	Marbled Teal	Vagrant
Netta rufina	Red-Crested Pochard	Vagrant
Aythya ferina	Pochard	WV
Aythya nyroca	Ferrugineous Duck	WV, RB
Aythya fuligula	Tufted Duck	WV
Hilvus nigrans	Black Kite	PM
Neophron percnopterus	Egyptian Vulture	Vagrant
Circaetus gallicus	Short-toed Eagle	Scarce, WV
Circus aeruginosus	Marsh Harrier	WV
Circus cyaneus	Hen Harrier	PM
Circus macrourus	Pallid Harrier	PM
Accipiter nisus	Sparrowhawk	WV
Buteo rufinus	Long-legged Buzzard	Scarce, WV
Aquila clanga	Spotted Eagle	PM
Aquila nipalensis	Steppe Eagle	Scarce, PM
Hieraaetus pennatus	Booted Eagle	Rare, PM
Pandion haliaetus	Osprey	RB
Falco naumanni	Lesser Kestrel	PM
Falco tinnunculus	Kestrel	WV
Falco columbarius	Merlin	Vagrant
Falco subbuteo	Hobby	PM
Falco concolor	Sooty Falcon	MB
Falco biarnicus	Lanner	Vagrant
Falco cherrug	Saker	Rare, PM

Ardea purpurea

Podiceps nigricolis

Aythya ferina

Anas acuta

NATURAL HISTORY

Species		Status
Latin Name	**Common Name**	
Falco peregrinus	Peregrine	?WV
Coturnix coturnix	Quail	PM
Rallus aquaticus	Water Rail	?PM
Porzana porzana	Spotted Crake	Scarce, PM
Porzana parva	Little Crake	Rare, PM
Porzana pusilla	Baillon's Crake	Rare, PM
Crex crex	Corncrake	Rare, PM
Gallinula chloropus	Moorhen	RB
Fulicula atra	Coot	RB, WV
Grus grus	Common Crane	Rare, PM
Chlamydotis undulata	Houbara Bustard	? Rare, WV
Haematopus ostralegus	Oystercatcher	WV
Himantopus himantopus	Black-winged Stilt	RB, PM
Recurvirostra avosetta	Avocet	WV, CB
Dromas ardeola	Crab Plover	PM
Burhinus oedicnemus	Stone Curlew	PM
Cursorius cursor	Cream-coloured Courser	RB
Glareola pratincola	Collared Pratincole	PM
Glareola nordmanni	Black-winged Pratincole	PM
Charadrius dubius	Little-Ringed Plover	PM, ?MB
Charadrius hiaticula	Ringed Plover	WV, PM
Charadrius alexandrinus	Kentish Plover	RB, PM
Charadrius mongolus	Lesser Sand Plover	WV, PM
Charadrius leschenaultii	Greater Sand Plover	WV, PM
Charadrius asiaticus	Caspian Plover	PM
Pluvialis dominica	Lesser Golden Plover	PM
Pluvialis squatarola	Grey Plover	WV
Hoplopterus indicus	Red-Wattled Plover	Vagrant
Chettusia gregaria	Sociable Plover	Vagrant
Chettusia leucura	White-tailed Plover	PM
Vanellus vanellus	Lapwing	WV
Calidris alba	Sanderling	PM
Calidris minuta	Little Stint	WV, PM
Calidris temminckii	Temminck's Stint	PM, WV
Calidris ferruginea	Curlew Sandpiper	PM
Calidris aloina	Dunlin	WV, PM
Limicola falcinellus	Broad-billed Sandpiper	PM
Philomachus pugnax	Ruff	WV, PM
Lymnocryptes minutus	Jack Snipe	WV
Gallinago gallinago	Common Snipe	WV
Limosa limosa	Black-tailed Godwit	PM
Limosa lapponica	Bar-tailed Godwit	WV
Numenius phaeopus	Whimbrel	PM
Numenius arquata	Curlew	WV
Tringa erythropus	Spotted Redshank	PM
Tringa totanus	Redshank	WV
Tringa stagnatilis	Marsh Sandpiper	PM, WV
Tringa nebularia	Greenshank	WV
Tringa ochropus	Green Sandpiper	PM, ?WV
Tringa glareola	Wood Sandpiper	PM, WV
Xenus cinereus	Terek Sandpiper	PM, WV
Actitis hypoleucos	Common Sandpiper	PM, WV
Arenaria interpres	Turnstone	PM, ?WV
Phalaropus lobatus	Red-necked Phalarope	PM
Stercorarius pomarinus	Pomarine Skua	Scarce, PM
Stercorarius parasiticus	Arctic Skua	Scarce, PM
Larus hemprichii	Sooty (Hemprich's) Gull	PM
Larus ichthyaetus	Great Black-headed Gull	PM

NATURAL HISTORY

Species		Status
Latin Name	**Common Name**	
Larus ridibundus	Black-headed Gull	WV
Larus genei	Slender-billed Gull	WV
Larus canus	Common Gull	Vagrant
Larus fuscus	Lesser Black-backed Gull	WV
Larus argentatus	Herring Gull	WV
Gelochelidon nilotica	Gull-billed Tern	WV, PM
Sterna caspia	Caspian Tern	RB, WV
Sterna bergii	Swift Tern	PM
Sterna bengalensis	Lesser Crested Tern	PM, ?MB
Sterna sandvicencis	Sandwich Tern	PM
Sterna hirundo	Common Tern	PM
Sterna repressa	White-cheeked Tern	?MB
Sterna anaethetus	Bridled Tern	MB
Sterna albifrons	Little Tern	PM
Sterna saundersi	Saunders' Little Tern	MB
Chlidonias hybridus	Whiskered Tern	PM
Chlidonias leucopterus	White-winged Black Tern	PM
Streptopelia decapcto	Collared Dove	?ST
Streptopelia turtur	Turtle Dove	PM
Streptopelia senegalensis	Palm Dove	RB
Oena capensis	Namaqua Dove	?ST
Psittacula krameri	Rose-ringed Parakeet	?RB, WV
Clamator glandarius	Great Spotted Cuckoo	Rare, PM
Cuculus canorus	Cuckoo	PM
Tyto alba	Barn Owl	RB
Otus scops	Scops Owl	PM
Bubo bubo	Eagle Owl	?
Athene noctua	Little Owl	?RB
Asio otus	Long-Eared Owl	Vagrant
Asio flammeus	Short-Eared Owl	Rare, WV
Caprinulgus europaeus	European Nightjar	PM
Caprinulgus aegyptius	Egyptian Nightjar	PM
Apus apus	Swift	PM
Apus pallidus	Pallid Swift	PM
Apus nelba	Alpine Swift	Scarce, PM
Alcedo atthis	Kingfisher	WV
Ceryle rudis	Pied Kingfisher	Vagrant
Merops orientalis	Little Green Bee-Eater	Vagrant
Merops superciliosus	Blue-Cheeked Bee-Eater	PM
Merops apiaster	European Bee-Eater	PM
Coriacias garrulus	European Roller	PM
Coriacias bengalensis	Indian Roller	Vagrant
Upupa epops	Hoopoe	PM
Jynx torquilla	Wryneck	PM
Eromopterix nigriceps	Black-Crowned Finch Lark	RB
Ammomanes cincturus	Bar-tailed Desert Lark	?ST
Ammomanes deserti	Desert Lark	RB
Alaemon alaudipes	Hoopoe Lark	RB
Melanocorypha calandra	Calandra Lark	Vagrant
Melanocorypha bimaculata	Bimaculated lark	PM
Calandrella brachydactyla	Short-toed Lark	PM, ?WV
Calandrella rufescens	Lesser Short-toed Lark	WV
Galerida cristata	Crested Lark	RB
Alauda arvensis	Skylark	?WV
Riparia riparia	Sand Martin	PM
Ptynoprogne rupestris	Crag Martin	PM
Hirundo rustica	Swallow	PM
Hirundo daurica	Red-Rumped Swallow	PM
Oelichon urbica	House Martin	PM
Anthus campestris	Tawny Pipit	PM, WV
Anthus trivialis	Tree Pipit	PM
Anthus pratensis	Meadow pipit	WV
Anthus cervinus	Red Throated Pipit	PM
Anthus spinoletta	Water Pipit	WV
Motacilla flava	Yellow Wagtail	PM
Motacilla citreola	Citrine Wagtail	Rare, PM
Motacilla cinerea	Grey Wagtail	PM

Sterna caspia

Coriacias garrulus

Ammomanes deserti

Galerida cristata

NATURAL HISTORY

Species		Status
Latin Name	**Common Name**	
Motacilla alba	White Wagtail	WV
Pycnopterus leucogenys	White-Cheeked Bulbul	RB
Hypocolius amoelinus	Hypocolius	Rare, WV
Cercotrichas galactotes	Rufous Bush Chat	PM, MB
Erithacus rubecula	Robin	Rare, WV
Luscinia luscinia	Thrush Nightingale	Rare, PM
Luscinia megarhynchos	Nightingale	PM
Luscinia svecica	Bluethroat	WV
Irania gutturalis	White-Throated Robin	PM
Phoenicurus erythronotus	Eversmann's Redstart	Rare, PM
Phoenicurus ochruros	Black Redstart	PM, ?WV
Phoenicurus phoenicurus	Redstart	PM, ?WV
Saxicola rubetra	Whinchat	PM
Saxicola torquata	Stonechat	WV
Oenanthe isabellina	Isabelline Wheatear	PM
Oenanthe oenanthe	Northern Wheatear	PM
Oenanthe pleschanka	Pied Wheatear	PM
Oenanthe hispanica	Black-Eared Wheatear	PM
Oenanthe deserti	Desert Wheatear	WV
Oenanthe xanthooprymna	Red-Tailed Wheatear	PM
Oenanthe lugens	Mourning Wheatear	WV
Oenanthe monacha	Hooded Wheatear	Scarce, WV
Oenanthe alboniger	Hume's Wheatear	Vagrant
Oenanthe leucopyga	White-Crowned Black Wheatear	Vagrant
Monticola saxatilis	Rock Thrush	PM
Monticola solitarius	Blue-Rock Thrush	PM
Turdus aerula	Blackbird	Vagrant
Turdus ruficollis	Black-Throated Thrush	WV
Turdus philomaelos	Song Thrush	WV
Turdus viscivorus	Mistle Thrush	Vagrant
Locustella luscinioides	Savi's Warbler	PM
Acrocephalus scirpaceus	Reed Warbler	PM
Acrocephalus arundinaceus	Great Reed Warbler	PM
Hippolais pallida	Olivaceous Warbler	PM
Hippolais languida	Upcher's Warbler	PM
Sylvia mystacea	Menetries' Warbler	PM
Sylvia nana	Desert Warbler	WV
Sylvia hortensis	Orphean Warbler	PM
Sylvia nisoria	Barred Warbler	PM
Sylvia curruca	Lesser Whitethroat	PM, ?WV
Sylvia minuta	Desert Lesser Whitethroat	?WV
Sylvia communis	Common Whitethroat	PM
Sylvia borin	Garden Warbler	PM
Sylvia atricapilla	Blackcap	PM
Phylloscopus sibilatrix	Wood Warbler	Rare, PM
Phylloscopus collybita	Chiffchaff	WV, PM
Phylloscopus trochilus	Willow Warbler	PM
Muscicapa striata	Spotted Flycatcher	PM
Ficedula parva	Red-Breasted Flycatcher	PM
Ficedula semitorquata	Semi-Collared Flycatcher	PM
Oriolus oriolus	Golden Oriole	PM
Lanius isabellinus	Isabelline Shrike	PM, WV
Lanius collurio	Red-Backed Shrike	PM
Lanius vittatus	Bay-Backed Shrike	Vagrant
Lanius minor	Lesser Grey Shrike	PM
Lanius excubitor	Great Grey Shrike	PM
Lanius senator	Woodchat Shrike	PM
Lanius nubicus	Masked Shrike	PM
Corvus ruficollis	Brown-necked Raven	?ST
Sturnus vulgaris	Starling	WV
Sturnus roseus	Rose-coloured Starling	Vagrant
Passer domesticus	House Sparrow	RB
Petronia brachydactyla	Pale Rock Sparrow	Scarce, PM
Euodice malabarica	Indian Silverbill	?ST
Fringilla montifringilla	Brambling	Vagrant
Carpodacus erythrinus	Common Rosefinch	Vagrant

Table 5: Reptiles of Qatar
(after M.B.H. Mohammed)

1. TURTLES

Chelonia mydas	Green Turtle
Eretmochelys imbricata	Hawksbill Turtle
Dermochelys coriacea	Leathery Turtle

2. LIZARDS

Geckonidae

Stenodactylus slevini	Slevin's Ground Gecko
Hemidactylus flaviviridis	Yellow-bellied House Gecko
Bunopus tuberculatus	Nocturnal Ground Lizard
Gymnodactylus scaber	Keeled Rock Gecko

Agamidae

Agama savignyi	Savigny's Agamid
Agama sinaita	Sinai Agamid
Uromastix microlepis	Small-scaled Dhabb
Phryocephalus nejdensis	Toe-headed Agamid

Varanidae

Varanus griseus	Desert Monitor

Amphisbaenidae

Diplometopon zarudnyi	Arabian worm lizard

Lacertidae

Acanthodactylus boskianus	Bosc's sand lizard
Eremias brevirostris	Short-nosed lizard

Scincidae

Mabuya aurata	Golden skink
Scincus scincus	Skink
Chalcides ocellatus ocellatus	Ocellated skink

3. SNAKES

Colubridae

Coluber ventromaculatus	Rat snake
Psammophis schokari	Hissing sand snake
Malpolon moilensis	Arabian rear-fanged snake
Lytorhynchus diadema	Leaf-nosed snake

Elapidae

Hydrophis cyanocinctus	Blue-banded sea-snake

Viperidae

Cerastes cerastes	Horned viper

Reptiles.

Qatar's reptiles, mostly in the form of lizards, have been the subject of a recent study carried out by Dr M.B.H. Mohammed, a member of the Zoology Department at Qatar University. In all, six hundred and ten reptiles were studied comprising twenty-seven species belonging to twenty-five genera. Prior to his study there was no scientific investigation of Qatar's reptiles. Table 5 provides a summary of recorded species.

Dr Mohammed's study effectively extends the known distribution of several species such as *Agama savignyi* (eastern Egypt to Palestine), *Scincus scincus* (northeastern Africa), and *Chalcides ocellatus* (north Africa to Palestine). Sea snakes and turtles are widespread in the western Indian Ocean and Gulf with the latter providing a particularly suitable habitat for several species. In a recently published study of the diets of some Qatari lizards (M.B.H. Mohammed 1987) Dr Mohammed noted that the main item of food is small arthropods with the exception of *U.microlepis* and *C.ocellatus* which ingest significant amounts of plant material. *S.scincus* and *A.scutellus* were found to have eaten small vertebrates together with numerous beetles and insect larvae. Nocturnal geckoes such as *Hemidactylus flaviviridis* had the highest intake of Diptera while *B.tuberculatus* and *G.scaber* had a main diet of ants and termites.

A commercial catch of the popular carangid or 'queenfish' *Scomberoides commersonianus* from Qatar's coastal waters which abound in fish. (*Vine*).

Marine Life

Hydrography

Hydrographic conditions in the western Gulf have been investigated by Hassan and Mahmoud from the Marine Sciences Department at the University of Qatar (Qatar University Science Bulletin, 1986, 6: 349–362). Measurements were made of sea water temperatures and salinities at various depths and during different seasons. Their results showed that inshore waters of the western Gulf during winter-time were vertically almost homogenous, whilst a weak stratification occurs in summer and early autumn. Oceanographic measurements around the peninsula of Qatar were carried out by Ali Beltagy, also from the Marine Science Department at Qatar University (Qatar University Science Bulletin, 1983, 3: 329–341). He plotted salinity, temperature and current speeds during four cruises carried out in 1979 and 1980. His work showed that salinity levels were highest near the coast where for example readings of 45 ppt were taken off Doha contrasting with 40.4 at Halul island. West of the peninsula, from the Gulf of Salwa northwards, salinities were considerably higher, reaching 58 ppt at Abu Samra but dropping to 53ppt off Dukhan, and progressively decreasing north of there. Winter sea-temperatures offshore ranged between 20 and 22 degrees centigrade with much cooler water, sometimes as low as 15 degrees

NATURAL HISTORY

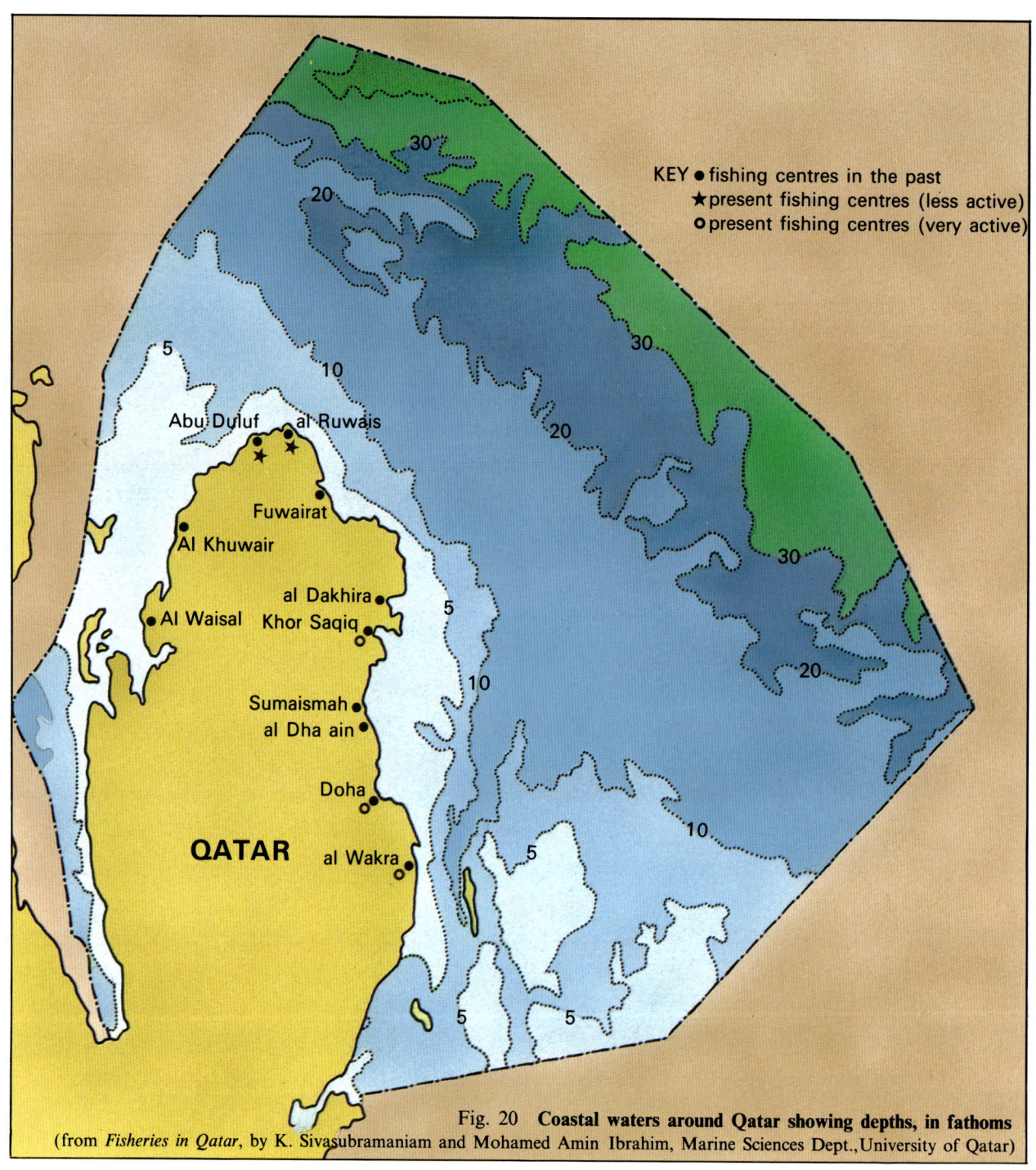

Fig. 20 Coastal waters around Qatar showing depths, in fathoms
(from *Fisheries in Qatar*, by K. Sivasubramaniam and Mohamed Amin Ibrahim, Marine Sciences Dept., University of Qatar)

centigrade, occurring in coastal shallows. Commenting upon water currents Beltagy states:- "The most conspicuous trend was a surface current, moving almost parallel to the coast; the width of this stream became narrower to the south, where it was restricted to the coastal 7km south of Doha....The current speed at the 0.5m depth was between 4.7cm/sec and 58.1 cm/sec.".

Sea creatures

Commercial marine resources of Qatar's coastal waters may be conveniently split into three categories, i.e. edible fish (both demersal and pelagic species); shrimps and pearl oysters. As we have seen in chapter one, the latter once formed the mainstay of the entire economy, but are hardly exploited today. Several studies have been carried out on the country's marine-life but for the visitor or resident wishing to gain an overall impression of the tremendous abundance of sea-creatures occuring in Qatari waters there is no better way that to visit the superb marine aquarium at Qatar's National Museum. An interesting study of demersal fish, based upon data collected from the F.A.O. Fishery Resources Survey (1975–79), has been completed by Sivasubra-

NATURAL HISTORY

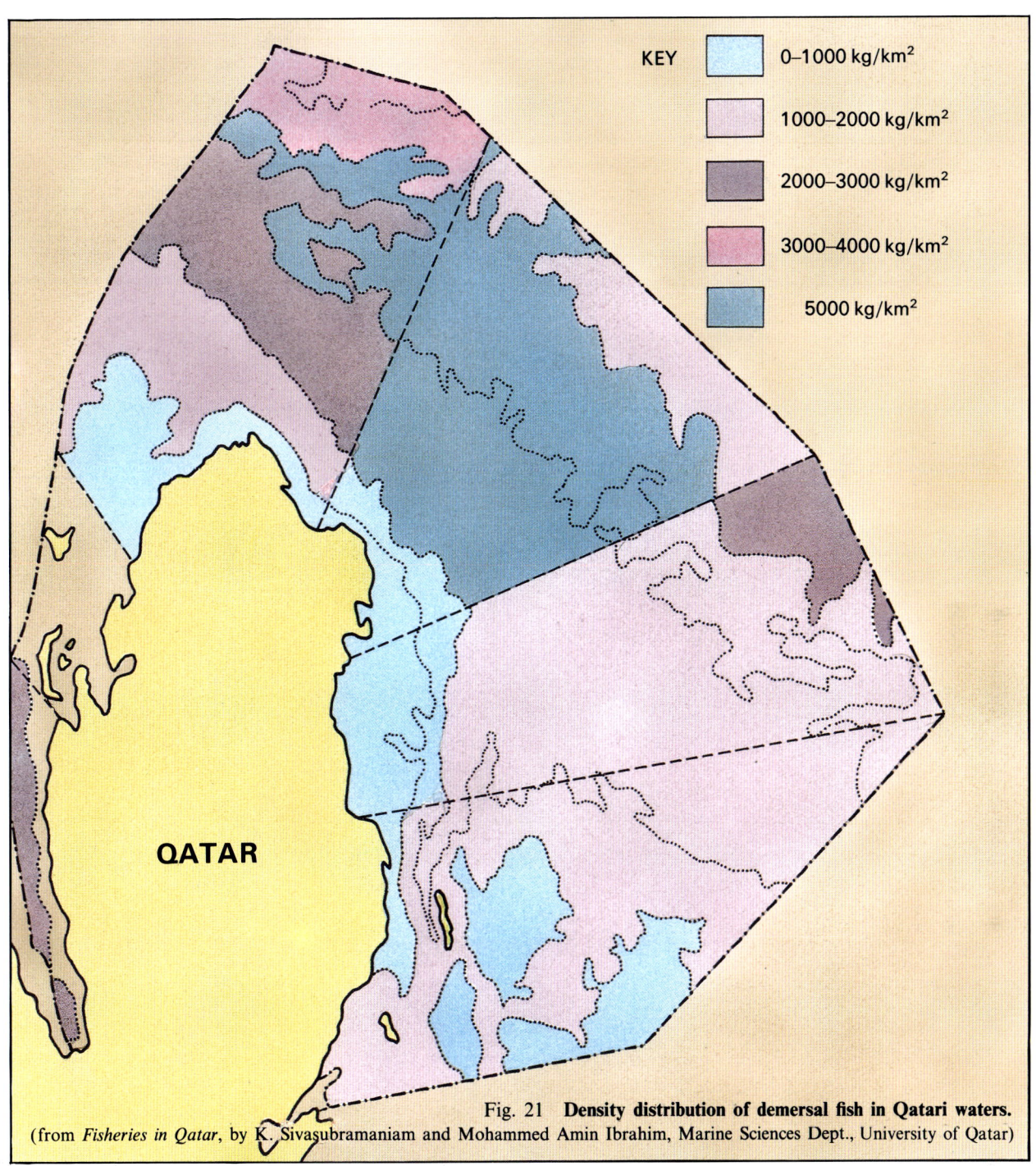

Fig. 21 **Density distribution of demersal fish in Qatari waters.**
(from *Fisheries in Qatar*, by K. Sivasubramaniam and Mohammed Amin Ibrahim, Marine Sciences Dept., University of Qatar)

maniam and Ibrahim (i.e. Demersal Fish Resources around Qatar: Qatar University Science Bulletin, 1982, 305–349). About a hundred and fifty species were identified during the survey and these belonged to around fifty families. Fig. 22 shows the density distribution of commercially valuable demersal fish in Qatari waters. As the figure indicates, richest fishing grounds are situated to the north-east of Qatar where the catch consists primarily of various carangids (jacks), Pomadasyidae (sweetlips), Lethrinidae (emperors) and Lutjanidae (snappers) together with lesser quantities of goatfish, shark, groupers, barracudas, threadfins, lizardfish, and rabbitfish. It has been estimated that the total biomass for demersal species around Qatar is 97,800 metric tons while the annual production of the fishery was estimated at 2,900 metric tons, nearly all of which comes from the eastern side of Qatar where Al Khor is a major fishing base. Theoretical calculations suggest that present annual landings fall far below the maximum sustainable yield from the fishery (ie c.17,000 tons of commercial demersal fish per year). Table 6 provides a list of common, scientific and local names for demersal fish caught in Qatari waters.

Table 6: Demersal Fish in Qatari Waters
(after Sivasubramaniam et al 1982)

Scientific Name	Common Name	Gulf Name
ARIIDAE		
Arius thalassinus	Sea catfish	Chem
ACANTHURIDAE		
Acanthurus lineolatus	Surgeonfish	Jeen
ARIOMMMIDAE		
Ariomma indica	Indian driftfish	Bankarah
BALISTIDAE		
Abalistes stellaris	Starry triggerfish	Homara
BOTHIDAE		
Bothus pantherinus	Leopard flounder	Khawfaah
Pseudorhombus arsius	Large tooth Flounder	Khawfaah
CAESIONIDAE		
Caesio coerulaureus	Gold banded Fusilier	
CARANGIDAE		
Alepes mate	Crevalle	
Carangoides bajad	Yellow spot cavalla	Korary
Carangoides malabaricus	Malabar cavalla	Zobaidy
Carangoides fulvoguttatus	Cavalla	
Carangoides ferdau	Ferdau's cavalla	Farkh el-jib
Caranx ignobilis	Yellowfin jack	
Caranx sem	Jack	
Caranx sexfasciatus	Dusky jack	
Decapterus kiliche	Scad	Sadah
Gnathodon speciosus	Toothless trevally	Rabib
Scomberoides commersonianus	Queenfish	Bisar
Selar crumenophthalmus	Bigeye scad	Dordoman
Selaroides leptolepis	Yellow stripe trevally	
Seriolina nigrofasciata	Black-banded trevally	Haman
Trachinotus blochii	Snub-nosed pompano	
Trachurus indicus	Horse mackerel	
CARCHARINIDAE		
Carcharias palasorrah	Grey dog shark	Gargoor
CHIROCENTRIDAE		
Chirocentrus dorab	Dorab wolf herring	Hoff
CHAETODONTIDAE		
Chaetodon melapterus	Butterflyfish	Anfooz
Chaetodon obscurus	Dark butterflyfish	Anfooz
Chaetodon vagabunda	Vagabond Coralfish	Anfooz
Heniochis acuminatus	Pennant Coralfish	
DASYATIDAE		
Himanture uarnak	Leopard ray	
FISTULARIDAE		
Istularia villosa	Flute mouth	Hakool
GERREIDAE		
Gerres filamentosus	Whipfin mojarra	Bedh
Gerres oyena		Bedh
GYMNURIDAE		
Gymnura poecilura	Butterfly ray	
LABRIDAE		
Choerodon robustus	Robust wrasse	
LEIOGNATHIDAE		
Leiognathus bindus	Ponyfish	Sawayah
Leiognathus sp.	Ponyfish	Sawayah

NATURAL HISTORY

Scientific Name	Common Name	Gulf Name
LETHRINIDAE		
Lethrinus lentjan	Redspot emperor	Shery
Lethrinus elongatus	Longnose emperor	Soly
Lethrinus nebulosus	Spangled emperor	Shery
Lethrinus kallopterus	Orange spotted emperor	Shery
LUTJANIDAE		
Lutjanus lineolatus	Yellow-striped snapper	Niser
Lutjanus malabaricus	Malabar snapper	Niser
Lutjanus sanguineus	Blood snapper	Niser
Lutjanus fulviflamma	Dory snapper	Niser
Lutjanus russelli	Russel's snapper	Hamra
Lutjanus johni	John's sea-perch	Niser
Lutjanus kasmira	Bluestripe snapper	Qazan
MONOCANTHIDAE		
Paramonacanthus choirocephalus	Pigface leather-jacket	Homara
Stephanolepis diaspros	Reticulated filefish	
MULLIDAE		
Parupeneus pleurotaenia	Goatfish	Sultan Ibrahim
Upeneus asymetricus	Goatfish	Sultan Ibrahim
Upeneus sulphureus	Yellow-striped goatfish	
Upeneus tragula	Dark-band goatfish	Sultan Ibrahim
MYLIOBATIDAE		
Aetomyleus nichofii	Eagle ray	
MURAENOSOCIDAE		
Muraenosox cinereus	Dogtooth pike conger	
NEMIPTERIDAE		
Nemipterus delagoae	Delagoae threadfin bream	Basy
Nemipterus tolu	Notched threadfin bream	Basy
Scolopsis bimaculatus	Two-spot monocle	
Scolopsis ruppelli	Monocle bream	Ebyeemy
Scolopsis ghanam	Monocle bream	Ebyeemy
ORECTOLOBIDAE		
Chiloscyllium grisseum	Carpet shark	
PLATYCEPHALIDAE		
Platycephalus indicus	Indian flathead	Thawr Amer
Platycephalus maculipinna	Spotted flathead	Thawr Amer
PLATACIDAE		
Platax orbicularis	Round batfish	
Platax teira	Longfinned batfish	
POMACANTHIDAE		
Pomacanthus maculosus	Yellowbar angelfish	
POMACENTRIDAE		
Abudefduf saxatilis vaigiensis	Sergeant major	Abudefduf
Dascyllus trimaculatus	Domino	
PLOTOSIDAE		
Plotosus anguillaris	Striped catfish	
POMADASYIDAE		
Plectorhynchus fangi	Sweetlip	Khobar
Plectorhynchus gaterinus	Gaterin	Kashrah
Plectorhynchus pictus	Painted sweetlip	Motawah
Plectorhynchus schotaf	Grey sweetlip	Yanamm
Plectorhynchus sordidus	Brown sweetlip	
Pomadasys multimaculatus	Blotched grunt	
Rhonciscus stridens	Banded grunt	Yemyam

Scolopsis ghanam

Lethrinus nebulosus

Lutjanus kasmira

Plectorhynchus gaterinus

NATURAL HISTORY

Scientific Name	Common Name	Gulf Name
PRIACANTHIDAE		
Priacanthus hamrur	Dusky-finned bigeye	
Priacanthus tayenus	Spot-finned bigeye	
RHINOBATIDAE		
Rhinobatus granulatus	Granulated shovelnose ray	Hariry
Rhynchobatus djiddensis	White-spotted shovelnose ray	Hariry
RHINOPTERIDAE		
Rhinopterus adspersa	Cow ray	
SCARIDAE		
Scarus ghobban	Bluebarred parrotfish	Jeyoon
SCORPAENIDAE		
Pterois russelli	Scorpionfish	Dajajah
SERRANIDAE		
Cephalopholis miniata	Coral grouper	Shninwa
Epinephelus areolatus	Areolated grouper	Qatmah
Epinephelus chlorostigma	Brownspotted grouper	Qatmah
Epinephelus jayakari	Whitespotted grouper	Hamoor
Epinephelus tauvina	Greasy grouper	Hamoor
Aethaloperca rogaa	Redmouth grouper	
SIGANIDAE		
Siganus canaliculatus	Whitespotted spinefoot	Safy
Siganus javus	Streaked spinefoot	Safy
SILLAGINIDAE		
Sillago sihama	Silver sillago	Hasoom
SOLEIDAE		
Synaptura orientalis	Oriental sole	Kharfaah
Pardachirus marmoratus	Moses sole	Mazlaqan
SPARIDAE		
Argyrops spinifer	Longspine seabream	Koofer
Diplodus kotschyi	Onespot seabream	Bent Nokhazah
Crenidens crenidens	Crenate tooth seabream	
Mylio bifasciatus	Porgy	Fasker
Mylio latus	Yellowfin seabream	Shaam
Pagellus sp.	Seabream	
Rhabdosargus sarba	Goldline seabream	
SPHYRAENIDAE		
Sphyraena jello	Banded barracuda	Dwelmi
Sphyraena obtusata	Obtuse barracuda	Swelmi
SYNODONTIDAE		
Saurida tumbil	Greater lizardfish	Hasoom
Saurida undosquamis	Brush-toothed lizardfish	
TETRADONTIDAE		
Chelonodon patoca	Gangetic blowfish	Fegl
Arothron stellatus	Starry blowfish	Fegl
THERAPONIDAE		
Pelates quadrilineatus	Trumpeter perch	
Therapon jarbua	Tiger bass	Zebah
Eutherapon theraps	Banded grunter	Zeeb
Autisthes puta		Zamroor
TORPEDINIDAE		
Torpedo marmoratus	Electric ray	

Scarus ghobban

Cephalopholis miniata

Epinephelus chlorostigma

Sphyraena jello

Rhabdosargus sarba

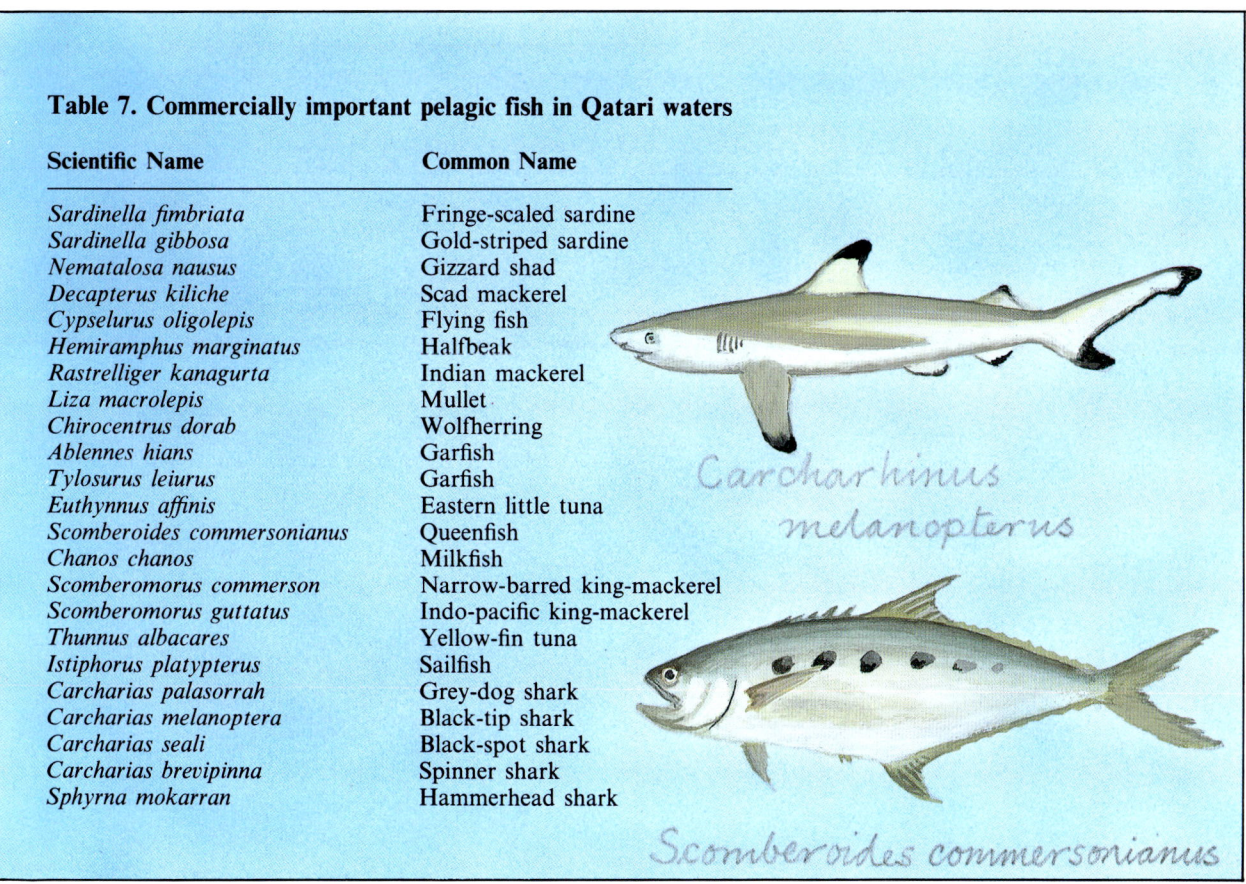

Table 7. Commercially important pelagic fish in Qatari waters

Scientific Name	Common Name
Sardinella fimbriata	Fringe-scaled sardine
Sardinella gibbosa	Gold-striped sardine
Nematalosa nausus	Gizzard shad
Decapterus kiliche	Scad mackerel
Cypselurus oligolepis	Flying fish
Hemiramphus marginatus	Halfbeak
Rastrelliger kanagurta	Indian mackerel
Liza macrolepis	Mullet
Chirocentrus dorab	Wolfherring
Ablennes hians	Garfish
Tylosurus leiurus	Garfish
Euthynnus affinis	Eastern little tuna
Scomberoides commersonianus	Queenfish
Chanos chanos	Milkfish
Scomberomorus commerson	Narrow-barred king-mackerel
Scomberomorus guttatus	Indo-pacific king-mackerel
Thunnus albacares	Yellow-fin tuna
Istiphorus platypterus	Sailfish
Carcharias palasorrah	Grey-dog shark
Carcharias melanoptera	Black-tip shark
Carcharias seali	Black-spot shark
Carcharias brevipinna	Spinner shark
Sphyrna mokarran	Hammerhead shark

The pelagic fishery is less developed than the demersal or bottom fishery. It is based upon migratory stocks of fish whose movements take them through Qatari waters as well as those of other Gulf states. Thus the population is effected by fishing efforts throughout the region rather than just in Qatar. The most important species in the catch are King Mackerel, *Scomberomorus commerson* and *S.guttatus*, but in addition to these a variety of other fish form the bulk of the "by-catch". Sivasubramaniam and Ibrahim have reported on this fishery (Qatar University Science Bulletin, Vol 3, 1983, pp. 297-326), concluding that the estimated potential sustainable yield is 2,200 metric tons per year. Their report includes a number of interesting analyses, too detailed to review here, and our list of commercially important pelagic fish is also drawn from this source.

Shrimps
The most important shrimp species in local catches, accounting for 95 percent of the haul, is *Penaeus semisulcatus*. These are fished mainly from July to December with catches averaging 16kg per artisinal boat per trip for those vessels fishing out of Doha and 27kg for those based at Al Khor. Recordings of annual catches show marked annual fluctuations with 76 tons landed by the artisinal fishery in 1980-81 (March to February). Commercial shrimp fishing in the Gulf has had a mixed history, Qatar became involved in 1968 and is now suffering from the general decline in stocks which led to a suspension of commercial fishing in 1979. More recently, controlled commercial fishing of shrimps has resumed and stocks are being more carefully managed than in the past. The inshore fishery is centred on an area of sea-bed between Doha and Al Khor, in the four to twelve metre belt. The fishery closely follows the seasonal migratory movements of *Penaeus semi sulcatus* with shrimps hugging the shallows early in the year and then gradually moving into deeper water. In addition to the main species of shrimp, the catch may include several other crustaceans including *Metapenaeus elegans*, *Metapenaeus stebbingi*, *Metapenaeus stridulans*, slipper lobsters (*Thenus orientalis*) and cuttlefish. Further particulars of Qatar's shrimp fishery are contained in a study by Sivasubramaniam and Ibrahim (Qatar University Science Bulletin,2(1), 1982, 265- 302), in a book by the same authors entitled Fisheries in Qatar (published by the Scientific Research Centre, University of Qatar, 1984), and in reports of the fisheries department.

NATURAL HISTORY

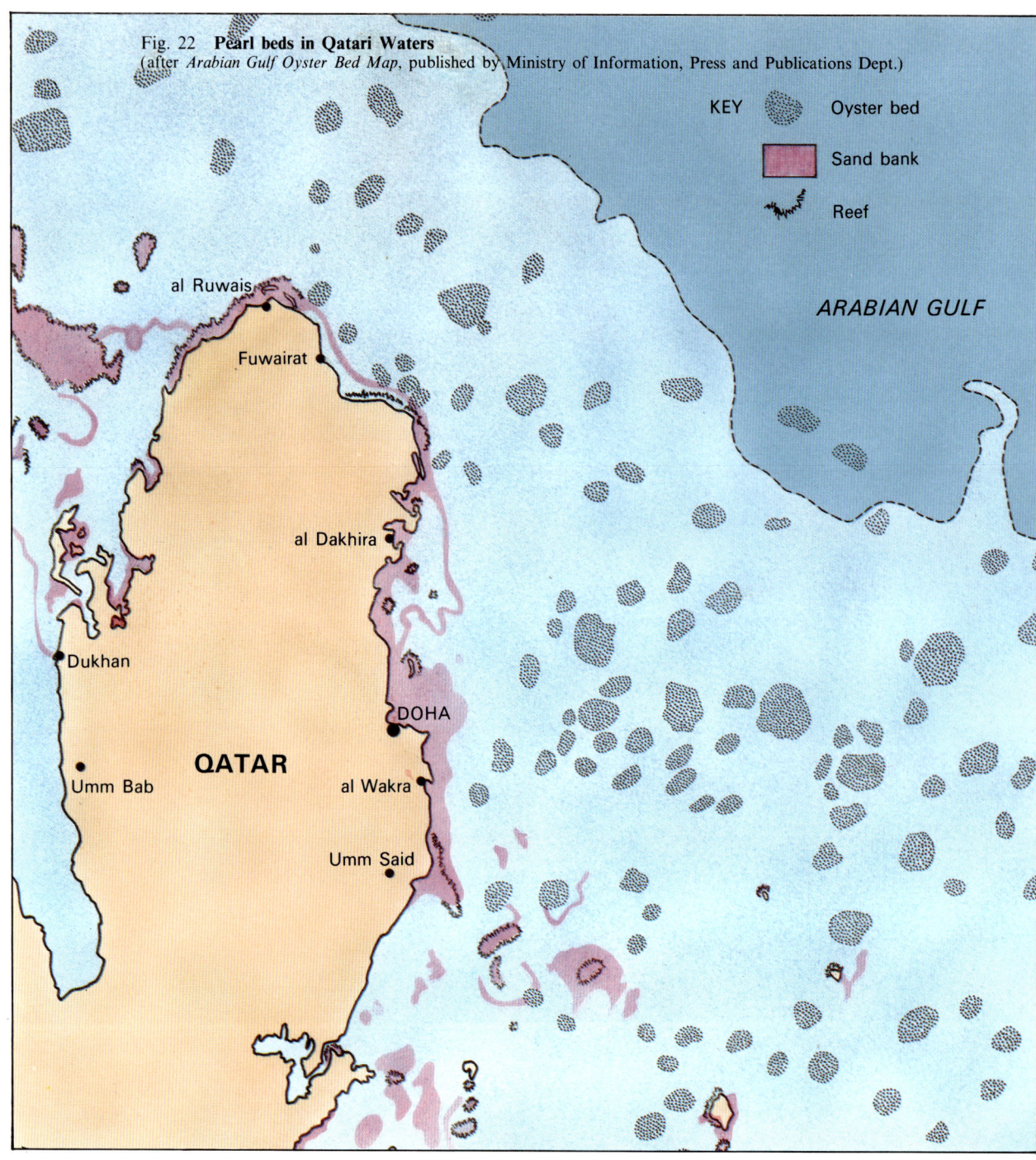

Fig. 22 **Pearl beds in Qatari Waters**
(after *Arabian Gulf Oyster Bed Map*, published by Ministry of Information, Press and Publications Dept.)

KEY
- Oyster bed
- Sand bank
- Reef

Pearl Oysters

The Arabian Gulf Oyster Bed Map, published by the Ministry of Information's Press and Publication Department in Doha, plots the positions of two hundred and six "hayrs" or oyster beds. The majority of these are around thirty miles offshore, inside the twenty-five fathom contour. Whilst each was known to fishermen by a distinct name, and was generally fished by the same divers, year after year, the beds were not generally regarded as belonging to any particular country or group of fishermen. The animal which proved to be such an attraction, at one time supporting the livelihoods of thousands of people throughout the Gulf, is a lowly molluscan bivalve with the high-sounding Latin name of *Pinctada margaritifera*.

The reproductive cycle of pearl-oysters commences with mass-spawning in spring when large quantities of eggs and sperm are released into the sea. Fertilised eggs then develop into planktonic larvae which feed primarily upon microscopic algae also drifting in the water-column. After three or four weeks the larvae are ready to settle and change their form to resemble young oysters. This settlement occurs in great numbers upon the leaves or blades of sea-grasses, especially *Halodule uninervis*. The pearl oyster spat remain attached throughout the summer but then, as autumn brings cooler waters and the sea-grasses begin to wither, the bivalves break off, fall to the ground and drift across the sea-bed until they encounter a hard substrate to which they attach with their byssal threads.

Qatar's pearl oyster fishery, like that of other Gulf countries, started to decline in the 1930's and is no longer operating on a commercial scale. The pearl oysters however are still present and it is quite possible that the future will bring a revival of pearl-fisheries both here and elsewhere in the region.

Shallow-water and intertidal marine environments around Qatar provide habitats for many other creatures. Available habitats have been classified by Price (1981) who reported on the echinoderms of the western Arabian Gulf, basing his analysis on earlier work in which he participated, culminating in publication of "Biotopes of the Western Arabian Gulf" (Basson et al, ARAMCO, 1977). Intertidal habitats can be broken up into exposed sandy beaches, sheltered mud-flats and rocky shores on which the hard substrate has been generally formed by beach-rock. Gastropod molluscs predominate in the intertidal although a variety of other groups occur here, especially in pools and under boulders. Mud flats tend to be highly productive, containing large numbers of polychaetes, gastropods, bivalves and decapods. Below tide level the seabed is generally formed by a mixture of sand and mud, and covered by sea-grasses or outcrops of weed covered rock, and coral platforms or reefs. One of the richest marine environments in Qatari waters are the submerged legs of oil and gas rigs situated offshore.

Mammals

Relatively little work has been carried out on Qatar's mammalian population. In a recent paper by Kamel and Madkour, (both members of the Zoology Department at the University of Qatar) some new records of Qatar mammals were presented (Qatar University Science Bulletin, 1984, 4: 125–128). Another recent study by Gamal Madkour (Zool.Anz.216 (1986) 1/2,S.72–80) reports on two species of bat and on the Red Fox. Their findings are summarised below. Larger terrestrial mammals such as the Arabian Oryx and Gazelle are not separately discussed here since they are mainly held in special reserves rather than still being present in the wild.

Grazing of desert range lands by herds of sheep and goats is a major problem for preservation of natural habitats in the desert. There is a strong case for controlling such herds. (*Ministry of Information and Culture*).

NATURAL HISTORY

Scimitar-horned oryx, *Oryx dammah*, were originally kept in captivity by the ancient Egyptians. It is a native of North Africa living in semi-desert areas, but has been extremely heavily hunted and is approaching extinction in the wild. Captive breeding in Qatar is helping to maintain the species gene pool. (*Ministry of Information and Culture*).

Sea-Cow: *Dugong dugong*

With the exception of whales which are occasional visitors to local waters, the sea-cow or Dugong is the largest of Qatar's resident mammals. Rarely seen alive, the shy mammal lacks the exuberance of dolphins and whales, never leaping out of the water, and seldom making even a splash as it submerges after inhaling. Its common name of "sea-cow" is particularly apt since it eats nothing but sea-grasses, thriving on the vast shallow "meadows" of marine angiosperms carpeting much of the Gulf's bottom. Once thought to be on the verge of extinction, hopes for its survival received a boost recently when a herd of 674 sea-cows was sighted over sea-grass beds not far north of the Qatar mainland.

Arabian Red Fox: *Vulpes vulpes arabica*

Whilst this is a widespread and not uncommon species in Qatar it is nevertheless rarely sighted. It is a versatile predator and farmers are always on their guard against marauding foxes which tend to live underground in day-time and emerge to hunt at night.

Ethiopian Hedgehog: *Paraechinus aethiopicus pectoralis*.

This is a nocturnal, somewhat reclusive hedgehog which may be found run-over on Qatar's inland roads. It is capable of running quite fast across the desert and is able to survive in very arid conditions.

Cape Hare: *Lepus capensis*
A specimen of this widely distributed hare was collected from the north of Qatar. Its distinctive long ears and well developed hind feet render it unmistakable. An adaptable species, the Cape Hare lives almost anywhere there is sufficient vegetation to support it, concealing itself by hiding in shallow excavated hollows in the sides of sandy hummocks.

Lesser Jerboa: *Jaculus jaculus vocator*
This species, distinguished by the presence of only three toes, together with tufts of stiff hair, on the hind foot, ranges from western Persia through the Arabian Peninsula and across the whole of north Africa. It lives in well constructed burrows under the sandy desert, and ranges out at night. Captive Jerboas do not drink but apparently derive all their moisture requirement from their food.

Arabian Gerbil: *Gerbillus nanus arabium*
This Gerbil is widespread in the Qatar desert where it may be observed at dawn and dusk, as well as during the night. It forms colonies on saline flats and semi-desert areas such as near the Salwa road, south of Doha and along the Doha to Dukhan road.

Cheesman's Gerbil: *Gerbillus cheesmani cheesmani*
This gerbil is widespread throughout Qatar's desert regions and was collected from the Salwa, Dukhan and Feyearat roads. Characteristic identification marks include a pale buff coloured back and hairy soles to its feet.

Trident Leaf-nosed Bat: *Asellia tridens tridens*
This bat is fairly widespread in Qatar, with small colonies inhabiting caves, old ruins and sometimes falaj water channels. They are frequently observed at dusk, flying low among palm groves or through gardens.

Hemprich's Long-eared Bat: *Otonycteris hemprichi*
A larger bat than the above species, it is also recognisable from its particularly large pointed ears. By no means as common as the trident leaf-nosed bat, four specimens were captured at Dahal El-Hamam, including three pregnant females (each with twins) and one male. It has a slow and "floppy" flight and appears to be well adapted to desert conditions.

ART AND ARTISTS

Arabian home *by Salman al Malki*

Art and Artists

Cloth design *by Haifa Abass*

ART AND ARTISTS

Girl's face *by Ahmed Abdullah*

ART AND ARTISTS

Clown *by Farig Idham*

ART AND ARTISTS

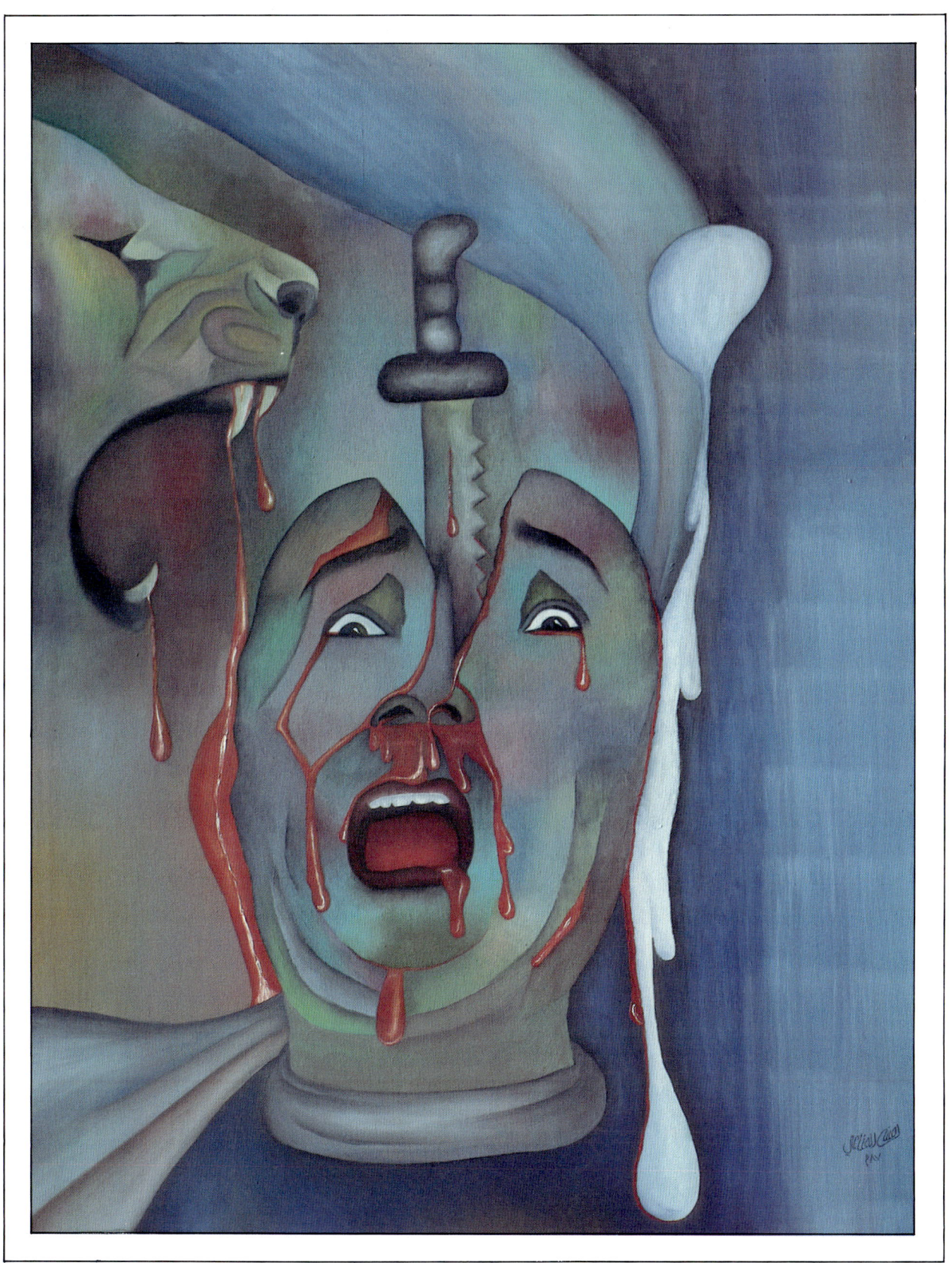

Surrealistic Nightmare *by Amina al Minnai*

111

ART AND ARTISTS

Fisherman and girl on beach *by Hissa el Merikh*

ART AND ARTISTS

Stone buildings in the desert *by Abdullah Dasmal*

ART AND ARTISTS

Balloons abstract *by Badria el Khobaisi*

Arabian architecture *by Wafiqa Sultan*

ART AND ARTISTS

Face of an Arabian man *by Rashid al Mohannadi*

ART AND ARTISTS

Face of Arabian girl *by Rashid al Mohannadi*

ART AND ARTISTS

Old man *by Issa al Maliki*

Fishermen with their nets *by Mariam Mohammed*

ART AND ARTISTS

Calligraphy and colours *by Ali Hassan*

ART AND ARTISTS

Weavers *by Maged Hilal*

ART AND ARTISTS

The Falconers *by Mohammed al Jida*

ART AND ARTISTS

The Dhow *by Mohammed Ali Abdullah*

ART AND ARTISTS

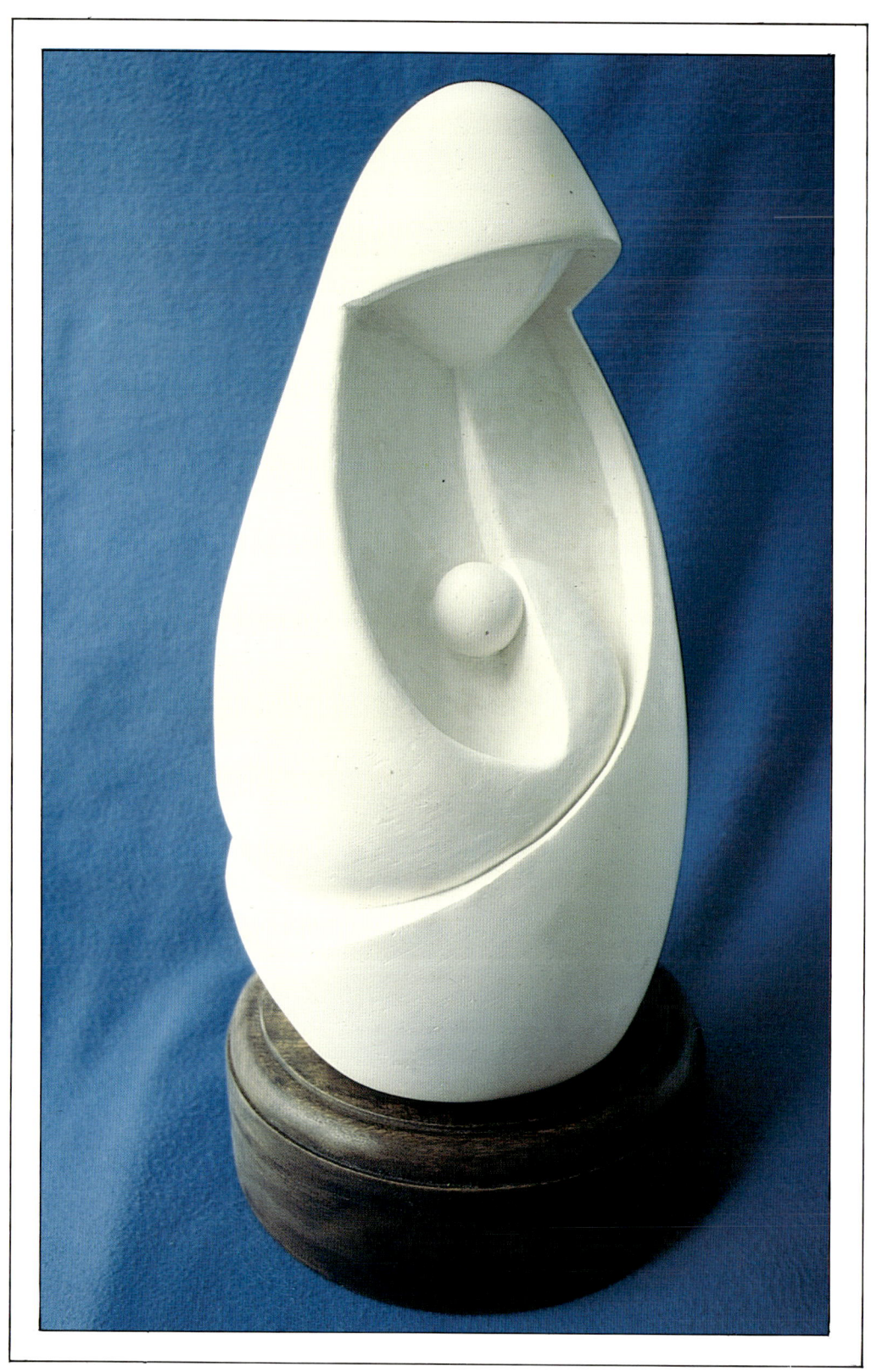

Mother and child sculpture *by Ahmed al Subai*

ART AND ARTISTS

Children of the world *by Nahed al Sulaiti*

ART AND ARTISTS

The Quest for our origins I *by Hassan al Mulla*

The Quest for our origins II *by Hassan al Mulla*

ART AND ARTISTS

The fort *by Ahmed Zainy*

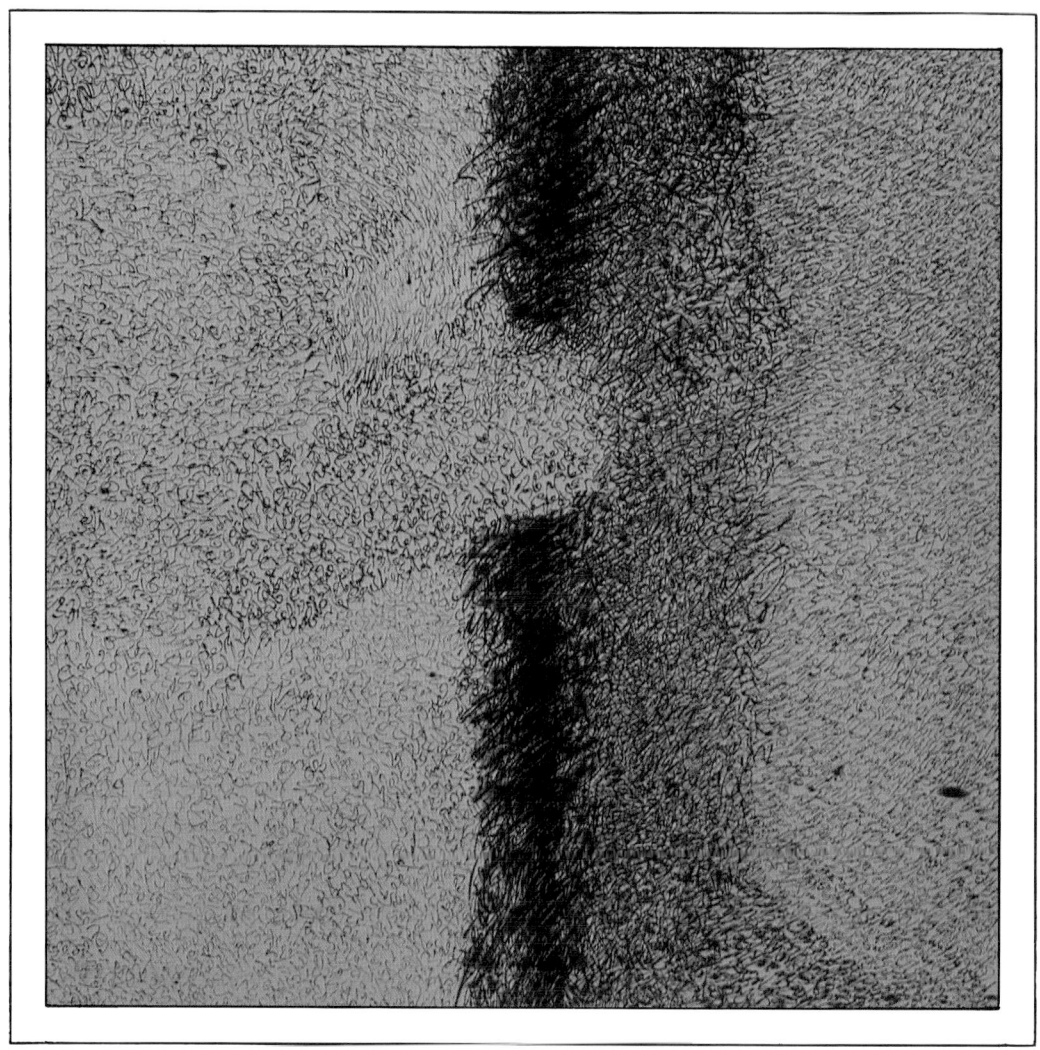

Abstract I *by Yousef Ahmed*

ART AND ARTISTS

Yousef Ahmed, the artist at work.

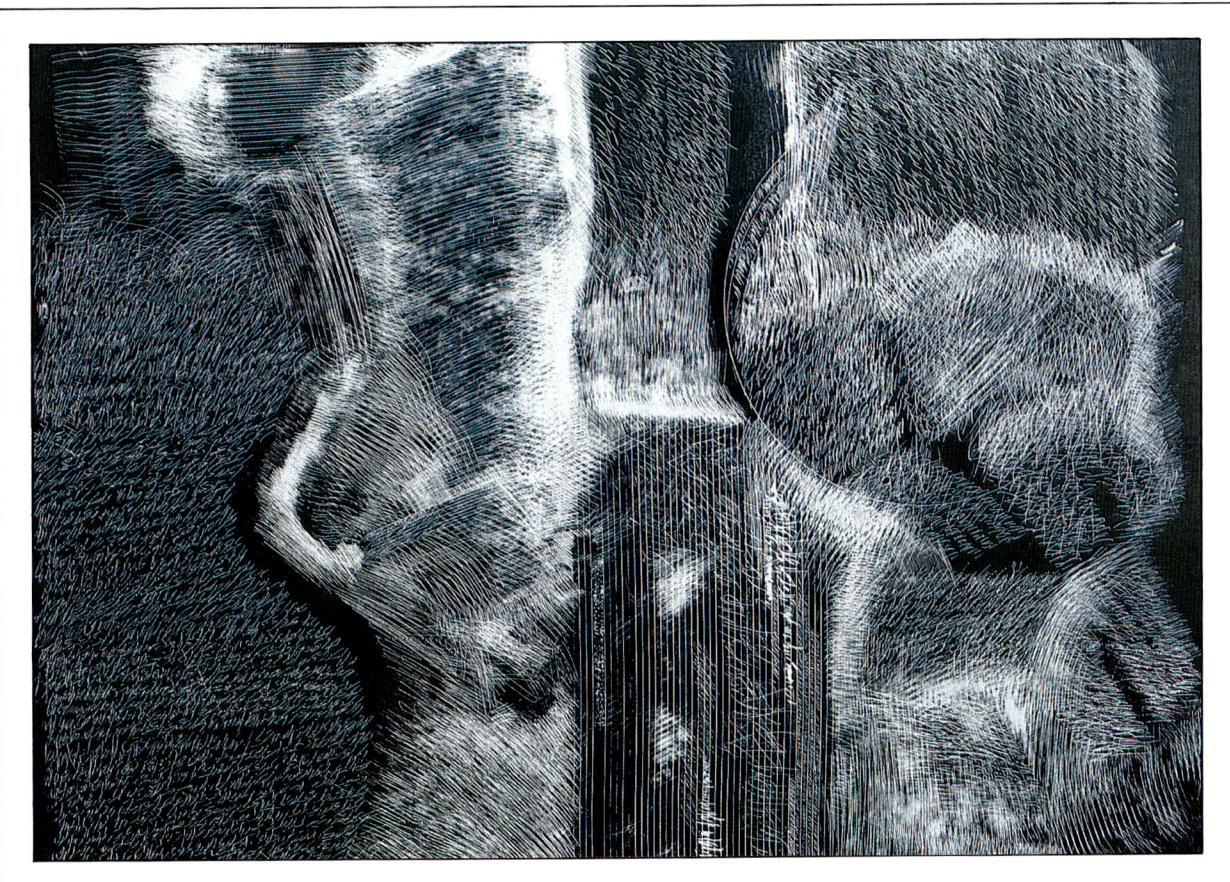

Abstract II *by Yousef Ahmed*

129

MODERN QATAR

Modern Qatar

The uninitiated visitor to Qatar, expecting to find a country locked into the past, will meet with a few surprises. Whilst Qatar values its traditions and has taken care to preserve many elements of its history, both the Government and its people are firmly attached to the present with a sharp eye upon planning for the future. In less than forty years this small nation has grown from dependence upon a dwindling pearling and trading economy to become an oil-rich country with one of the highest per-capita incomes in the world. Politically, Qatar is a sovereign independent Arab state in which Islam is the official religion and Islamic jurisprudence the principal source of law. Firmly committed to cooperation with other Arab states in tackling the region's development, Qatar is an active member nation of the Gulf Cooperation Council. Qatar's Head of State, or Emir, is H.H. Sheikh Khalifa bin Hamad Al-Thani, the supreme authority, who is assisted by a Council of Ministers over which he presides. In addition an Advisory Council, whose membership of thirty is drawn from prominent members of the community, plays a significant role in helping to shape policies.

Oil was first discovered in Qatar, at the Dukhan oil-field, in October 1939, close to the commencement of the Second World War: an event which prevented development of the find for six or seven years. Indeed, it was not until 1949 that oil was first exported from Umm Said's eastern terminal. Revenues finally began to flow and the country was gradually lifted out of a lingering state of economic depression. Despite this rather slow start, it was in fact one of the first Gulf countries to establish significant revenues from oil production. Qatar joined OPEC in 1961, the first non-founder member to do so.

In 1972 the Qatar National Petroleum Company was formed and was closely followed by establishment of the Qatar General Petroleum Corporation in July 1974, after OPEC's decision to raise the price of crude oil to a more equitable level. By 1977, all foreign equity in Qatar's oil companies had been purchased so that national development of the oil industry could proceed under the umbrella of the Qatar General Petroleum Corporation (QGPC). Initially oil production was centred on the Dukhan field in the west of the peninsula, but offshore oil and gas fields rapidly gained in importance, eventually surpassing onshore production in 1973. While there have been legitimate fears about the extent of Qatar's presently known oil reserves and how long they will last, with the year 2015 having been mooted, the situation with regard to other hydrocarbon energy resources is considerably more optimistic. The Natural Gas Liquids plant at Umm Said is able to draw upon a huge resource, including that of the North Field whose

Right: Gas liquefying plant at Umm Said. (*Ministry of Information and Culture*).

Opposite: Aerial view of Umm Said refineries and petrochemical plants, the hub of Qatar's oil-based economy. (*Ministry of Information and Culture*).

MODERN QATAR

Opposite, top: 'DANA' offshore drilling platform. (*Ministry of Information and Culture*).

Opposite, bottom: Onshore oil wells in the Dukhan region. (*Ministry of Information and Culture*).

Right: The petrochemical complex at Umm Said. (*Ministry of Information and Culture*).

Below: Abu Fontas Power Station supplies part of the county's needs for both electricity and water. (*Ministry of Information and Culture*).

discovery has raised estimates of Qatar's gas reserves to around a hundred trillion cubic feet; enough to keep the lights burning for a while yet!

Naturally enough industrial production in Qatar has focussed upon its hydrocarbon resources, with downstream products such as gasoline condensate, propane, butane, ethane-rich and methane-rich gases making the major contribution to earnings. Given such available low-cost energy the Government has encouraged development of local industries, leading to a diversification of the economy. A necessary prerequisite for such development has been establishment of an efficient infrastructure of facilities and services such as electricity, water, roads, ports and good telecommunications. Special industrial zones have also been built where all the necessary services are provided and where various companies have established their manufacturing headquarters. In addition to these physical support facilities the Qatar Government has paid close attention to the social welfare of its people, providing high quality health and education services and subsidised housing programmes.

Umm Said, situated on the south-east coast, about half an hour's drive from Doha, is the industrial heart of Qatar and it is here that most of the heavy industries are found. The site was originally chosen as a result of its proximity to deep navigable water, permitting the docking of large vessels. Pipe-lines from the Dukhan oil field terminate here and crude oil is exported via the modern port. Among the country's major industries, the National Oil Distribution Company (NODCO) is one of the largest, operating a new refinery, linked to an older unit at Umm Said,

Inside the iron and steel complex. (*Ministry of Information and Culture*).

which supplies all national demand for petroleum products and exports surplus products. The Qatar Chemical Fertiliser Company (QAFCO) produces ammonia and urea fertilisers and is jointly owned by the Qatar General Petroleum Company and Norsk Hydro: most of its high quality fertiliser products are exported to Asian markets. The Qatar Steel Company (QASCO) is another joint-venture operation, this time with Kobe Steel Ltd and Tokyo Boeki Ltd having a minority stake in the venture. The company produces sponge iron, steel and reinforcing rods for the local and regional construction industries. The Qatar Petrochemicals Company (QAPCO), 84% owned by the Qatar General Petroleum Corporation and 16 percent by CdF Chimie, uses ethane enriched gas from the Natural Liquids Gas Plants in the production of ethylene, sulphur and low density polyethylene primarily for export.

In addition to these projects the industrial base has been considerably broadened by creation of other medium and light manufacturing projects. The first non-oil national industry to be established in the country was for the manufacture of cement for local use by the Qatar National Cement Company. The project's aim was to reduce imports of cement and it has been largely successful in this objective. Local demand for flour and bread is also met through local manufacturing by the Qatar Flour Mills Company. The Industrial Development Technical Centre played a key role in establishing an organic fertilisers plant which converts urban refuse into fertilisers suitable for local agricultural use. In addition to these projects others cater for manufacture of detergents, automatic livestock slaughter in accordance with Islamic law, production of industrial gases, paints, dairy produce and various other goods.

Despite the size of such projects, Qatar does not give the impression of being industrialised. Concentration of petrochemical and manufacturing industries at centres such as Umm Said ensures that most of the country retains a more natural appearance. Nevertheless it is still difficult to move far from some form of development project, whether this be in the form of a new road, a line of power cables, a drainage swamp filled by desalinated water, or in the many urban improvements which have taken place, including schools, hospitals, ultra-modern office buildings, or Qatar's space-age university campus.

The University, established in 1973, is perhaps one of the best examples of how Qatar places emphasis on the importance of preparing and training its people for the challenges of modern

QATAR UNIVERSITY

life. Housed in an ultra-modern, brilliantly conceived series of buildings based on the traditional wind-tower cooling system, the university is a centre of research and education in all fields. In order to learn more about Qatar's education system I visited Dr Abdulla Juma Al Kobaisi, Acting President of this university. Recalling his own schooling in Qatar he explained how things were in his youth. *"At that time, around 1948 or 1949, I started in Kitab school. There were really two types of school available. In the city, in Doha, it was a semi-modern primary education and Kitab school while in the villages there was just Kitab schooling. From around 1952 onwards, gradually, the semi-modern education increased at primary level and they reorganised the primary education system. Around 1958 a secondary school was established in Doha. For my part, following the Kitab school, I attended primary school and later on an evening school. At that time many of the students who were furthering their education took evening classes since they had grown too old for primary school. The evening school began around 1955 and it ran in parallel with the day system. The education system in Qatar really began to expand at this time. This was due to many factors, the first of which was the money from oil, and there was a tremendous educational budget available. And then the call for education was deeply bound up with the religious call. Educational standards were spreading throughout the Gulf and Qatar was part and parcel of that process. The first "ministry" of education was in fact a committee. We call it a ministry because that is the terminology in use today, but it wasn't a ministry in the true sense. A committee was formed in 1952 to provide an impetus to the development of education in Qatar. And then, in 1957, Shaikh Khalifa was minister or supreme director of education, and he speeded the growth of education, guiding its development and overseeing the establishment of what we might regard as a regular system of education available to boys and girls."*

Education in Qatar brought inevitable changes to the social and economic fabric of the society. *"Actually you have two generations we can talk about. The generation who are born say, in 1910 or 1920, they lived in the pre-oil period and their lives were rich in culture; and on the other hand there are those who were born, say in the 1960's, growing up surrounded by the trappings of modern-life, television, nice schools, nice homes; they are really*

Computer education has become a compulsory part of the syllabus at Qatar University. (*Ministry of Information and Culture*).

Handcrafts are taught throughout school and also to adult classes. (*Ministry of Information and Culture*).

not familiar with the form of life which existed in Qatar before, and these people probably do not feel that there has been such a great change or shock to the way of life in Qatar. But for those who lived during the pearl-diving period, and are still living today, they refer to the past as a "golden era" for more than one reason. First of all they have lost their key role as the mainstay of the economy. Today's role is for those who have a chance to be educated whereas in the past most people's educational levels were the same, only their experience differed. Then these older folk yearn for the pearl diving days. This was not like ordinary fishing, the pearling was full of culture, it was quite special.."

I asked Dr Abdulla about his own feelings regarding Qatar's recent past and its rapid development. "*Well, for me, the change was not so remarkable because I lived through it. I did not see that there was a great jump. I moved with it. I was born in 1942 and remember how things were in the early fifties. But for my elder brothers and my parents, for them it is different. They remember how things were in the past, before oil, and they explain to us how at times it was harsh and yet at other times it was really beautiful. Still in Qatar, you can find both kinds of people, the older ones for whom these changes are not understandable and the newer generation who have moved with the changes. But we try to give the youth a feeling about the past. On weekends we might go to picnic at Al Jumayl, in the north, where we can try to explain to our children how life was in the past. We bridge the generation gap in this way. My mother describes to me and I explain to my children. It is a kind of fantasy, but it serves a useful purpose. It gives a feeling of belonging to a village for which today there is no function, whereas in the past it had a great importance.*"

My discussion with Dr Al Kobaisi gradually shifted ground from the past, from his own upbringing and feelings about the changes which have occurred, towards the present. I asked him whether he felt that rapid development had eroded the sense of national identity among Qataris. "*Well, I don't know if we can say there is a Qatari tradition which differs from the Gulf region as a whole. Some people have quite a narrow vision, focussing on just Qatar, just Bahrain, or just Kuwait, and they consider that these are big nations which can survive alone with their own traditions, but I don't think this is the case in the Gulf. If one speaks of the traditions of Bahrain for example, we must realise that a great*

MODERN QATAR

The future of Qatar rests with its young people who are receiving every benefit of modern education and are being well prepared for the years ahead. (*Ministry of Information and Culture*).

MODERN QATAR

MODERN QATAR

Students in a workshop at the Industrial Training Centre. (*Ministry of Information and Culture*).

deal of these traditions are shared equally by Qatar. However, if we take the Gulf as a whole, then we can recognise a distinct tradition and culture which may be regarded as particularly characteristic of it. This Gulf culture differs significantly from those of other countries like Egypt, Iraq or Syria. But for Qatar itself, comparing it with for example Bahrain, Kuwait, Oman or the Emirates, you may find just small differences, similar perhaps to being in England and noticing regional difference in accents and local traditions. If we are to characterise Qatar, Qatar is an Arabic and Islamic country; it belongs to the Arabic world as one of its nations, and this is written into the constitution. For the future, I think Qatar and the other Arab nations must be united to form bigger states. This is for the future. But still there will remain the small things associated with each individual country. There will always be a sense of belonging to one's homeland. We are moving along parallel lines, if you like, to the European Community. In our schooling, when we teach children about their environment for example, each country will have some differences, but when we teach about broader issues, about Islam, or about Arab teaching, it will be the same."

Dr Al Kobaisi is strongly involved in the University itself and in its planning. I asked him whether this took place in the context of a regional education policy. *"In some cases the faculties have been established to meet national needs. For example the Marine Sciences Department was set up to explore our coastal waters, to help to protect them from pollution and to discover any valuable resources which we may possess. Our educational faculty was set up to train teachers. We need teachers, there is no doubt about that, and the faculty is helping us to meet this need. But in the case of engineering for example, one has in mind two objectives in providing education to students of this faculty. First of all we need good scientists in engineering to understand the changes which are happening in the advanced world and to ease the transition of technology. Secondly, the other objective is for research to be carried out into problems facing engineers here in Qatar: buildings, roads, and so on. Thus we encourage engineering graduates to come back into the university so we may talk with them about the problems that are being faced.*

We have a special level of cooperation with the Gulf University. We do not need to duplicate expensive faculties within the region. If for instance there is a medical school in the Gulf University, then here we will hesitate to establish one, while there is an adequate faculty there. It would of course be fine to have all the faculties here in Qatar, but we must look at the cost effectiveness of such a programme. While we may have a few students who take medicine, why not send them to the Gulf University which we are supporting? Then we have the situation in our engineering faculty, where we are asked why we do not establish a Department of Petroleum. Our answer is that we shall not establish such a department when there is a perfectly adequate one at the Gulf University. We believe in this kind of coordination and cooperation within the region. Planning for such coordination of tertiary level education in the Gulf takes place at an annual meeting of presidents of the Gulf Universities where we can sit together and discuss how to avoid unnecessary duplication of our efforts."

Qatar University, under the presidency of Dr Abdulla Al Kobaisi has earned a high reputation for all levels of its activities and in 1986 a policy was laid down for a constant improvement in the quality of education within the university. "There are several reasons for this new emphasis", Dr Al Kobaisi explained. "First of all, the university was established fifteen years ago. At first we strove to establish the basic infrastructure of the university and to gain recognition for it at an international level. Then, after we moved to these excellent new buildings, we reviewed our progress. We are blessed with a good number of highly qualified staff but relatively few students. Finally we came to the realisation that we should not be continually focussing upon the quantity of students we teach. We had no problem about the quantity of students. What we needed to focus on was the quality of the education we provided. This was of course a hard mission. To enhance the quality of education within a university brings challenges to all: for the leaders of the university, for the staff, the students, and for the society as a whole. We are not focussing on just one aspect of the student personality, but we are focussing on the whole person including extracurricula activitities. Actually physical education is a

Khalifa Olympic Stadium can seat over 40,000 spectators and is a demonstration of the Government's strong support for sport and health training among Qataris. (*Ministry of Information and Culture*).

MODERN QATAR

MODERN QATAR

Opposite, top: Monitoring studio at Qatar Television. (*Ministry of Information and Culture*).

Opposite, bottom: The Doha Earth Satellite Station – a vital link in Qatar's ultra-modern communications network. (*Ministry of Information and Culture*).

Below: An operating theatre at Hamad General Hospital. (*Ministry of Information and Culture*).

compulsory part of the curriculum here and we have provided an excellent environment for this. We are also introducing computers as a university requirement for all students, regardless of what they are studying. In terms of a general improvement of quality within the university each faculty is working on this right now. Their efforts fall under two categories, firstly to strengthen the internal programme and secondly to seriously tailor this programme to meet the future needs of Qatar.

"*In addition to this we are introducing what is for Qatar a new form of education: technical training. This will provide the qualified technicians for the country. This technical education will be run by the university itself for three main reasons. Firstly economically, there is no sense in duplicating all the facilities we possess here for such an education to be provided from another base in Qatar. We have all the necessary facilities here, so why not use them? Secondly, for social reasons: even in advanced countries, there is a kind of stigma attached to technical education. We have no doubt however about the value and importance of technical education and for this reason we shall include it in the University. It is not lower or higher than the academic education we are already offering. It is simply different. Our third reason for putting the technical education programme within the University is to narrow the gap between the academician and the practical technician. We can live together in one environment, and we need to do that. I really believe this is very important. Theory and practice are after all inter-dependent. If we succeed in this kind of policy Qatar University will be among the very few who have adopted such a programme and I am convinced it is the way forward.*"

Qatar's educational programme is one of many examples of the country's incredible development since its ties with Britain were severed. The surprise announcement, in November 1968, that the British Government was pulling all its military personnel back from a line drawn east of Suez,

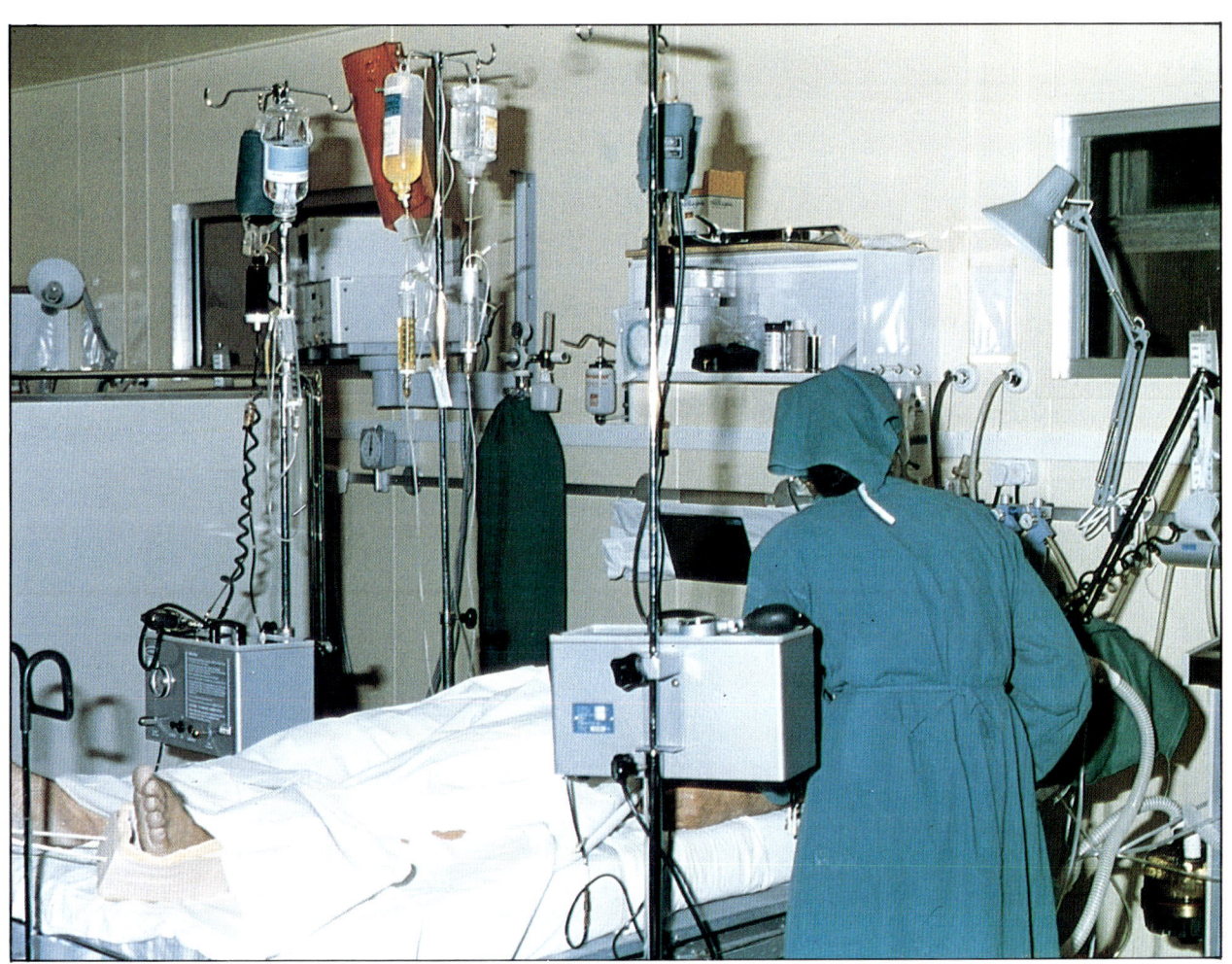

MODERN QATAR

Above: Doha port offers shipping the most up-to-date facilities. (*Ministry of Information and Culture*).
Opposite, top: Aerial view of the city of Doha. (*Ministry of Information and Culture*).
Opposite, bottom: The Emiri Diwan, Seat of Goverment of the State of Qatar. (*Ministry of Information and Culture*).

effectively terminated the old treaties of protection with the Gulf states. In the aftermath a federation of nine Gulf shaikhdoms, Bahrain, Qatar and the seven Trucial States, was initially considered, but negotiations towards this end proved very difficult. Qatar, early in 1971, promulgated a provisional constitution which set about crystallising the emergent nation, building on the traditional political structures already in place. Under the constitution Qatar is declared to be a sovereign independent Arab state whose regime is democratic. Although this particular concept of a nation was new, Qataris had long since felt the underlying threads of identity with one another and a deep felt loyalty to their tribal leader whose close relationship with his people was based on an unwritten code. The position of the Al Thani is confirmed by the constitution which lays down that the ruler, the head of state, shall always be a member of this family: succession, as in the past, is based on a consensus of notables. Although the ruler's legislative and executive powers are supreme, no longer can he be confused with the state of which he is now representative; ruler and state are from henceforth two separate entities.

The constitution also brought into being a Council of Ministers to "assist the Head of State in the discharge of his duties and the exercise of his powers." The Council "in its capacity as the highest executive organ of the State" is responsible for proposing draft laws, for implementing these laws and for supervising the financial and administrative affairs of the Government which now comprises fifteen Ministries: Defence, Education, Foreign Affairs, Economy and Trade, Justice, Electricity and Water, Emiri Diwan Affairs, Municipal Affairs and Agriculture, Interior, Finance and Petroleum, Industry and Public Works, Labour and Social Affairs and Housing, Transport and Communications, Public Health, and Information and Culture. A partly-elected Advisory Council, also decreed by the constitution and finally established in April of 1972, provides a forum for discussion of the Council of Minister's draft laws and proffers advice on other state matters.

Apart from the machinery of government, a few of the other clauses in the constitution are interesting, particularly because they reflect

MODERN QATAR

Left: Mosque minarette at Wakra. Religion continues to play a vital role in the lives of Qataris. (*Vine*).

Opposite, top: Jogging along the Doha corniche with Sheraton Hotel in background. (*Vine*).

Opposite, bottom: Marina in front of Gulf Hotel, Doha. (*Vine*)

Below: The Bismillah Restaurant remains something of a land-mark in central Doha since it was the city's first hotel. Its crumbling edifice is in sharp contrast to the ultra modern sophistication of the city's luxury hotels built in recent years. (*Vine*).

strongly-held traditional values. The constitution reiterates the traditional belief that the family is the nucleus of Qatari society and guarantees that the law will do all it can to safeguard its unity. Under the constitution, Islam is the religion of Qatar and the shariah law the basis for its legislation (the laws being implemented by a strongly independent judiciary). As far as social welfare is concerned the state guarantees under its constitution to provide everyone with medical care, both curative and preventative. The state also promises to implement measures to safeguard its citizens in illness, old age or disability.

On 11th September 1971 Qatar was admitted to the League of Arab States and its membership of the United Nations was ratified by that body's General Assembly on 21st of September in the same year. Although still a very new nation coming to terms with its modern constitutional framework Qatar, benefiting from a stable and wise leadership and thriving economy, has pursued a far-seeing foreign policy centred on strengthening links between Arab and Islamic states and defending the interests of Arabs everywhere. Qatar's firm stance on these issues has been underscored by its membership of the Co-operation Council for the Arab States of the Gulf (GCC) which was formed in 1981. The six states forming the GCC (Saudi Arabia, Kuwait, Bahrain, Qatar, the United Arab Emirates and Oman) do not confine themselves solely to the coordination of international affairs, members also cooperate on economic and security matters.

In this chapter we outline some of the enormous strides the state of Qatar has made in the few short years since it achieved the means to control its own destiny. Besides the installation of an efficient administrative structure unprecedented progress has also been made in industrial development; in agriculture; in health-care, housing, electricity, water supplies, roads and telecommunications; but above all in the field of education in which an ambitious programme is being implemented to ensure that young Qataris, the real wealth of the nation, can take their place in the modern world. All this has been achieved in a modest and careful manner, building on the strong foundations of the past and embracing social customs and traditions cherished by all Qataris.

Qatar's Central Statistical Organisation provides much of the necessary data to inform decision makers in Government and business about key parameters of the economy and of the social situation within the country. Some recent data on Qatar is presented in table 8.

MODERN QATAR

'Greening' of the desert and beautification of urban areas is a major priority of the Qatar Government which employs modern growing techniques in its agricultural development. (*Ministry of Information and Culture*)

Table 8. Statistical Summary

	1985	1986	1987	1988
Population		369,075	384,970	
Natural Increase	8431	9,158	9,131	
Gross Domestic Product (Q.R. Million)				
1. Agriculture & Fishing	213	237	241	243
2. Manufacturing	1770	1777	1847	2462
3. Electricity & Water	191	363	359	366
4. Building & Construction	1313	1054	1086	1015
5. Trade, Restaurants & Hotels	1186	1149	1172	1374
6. Transport & Communication	450	410	412	518
7. Finance, Insurance, Real Estate & Business Services	1899	1842	1958	2239
8. Social Services	201	214	216	217
9. Imputed Bank Service Charges	(−484)	(−553)	(−533)	(−540)
10. Govt. Services	5748	6047	5848	6900
11. Household Services	187	198	213	233
12. Import Duties	129	130	131	139
TOTAL	22398	18263	18580	20810

Industry Production
(Units = 1000 metric tonnes)

Propane & Butane	549	591	586	509
Ammonia & Urea	1383	1405	1416	1504
Organic Fertilisers	22	21	28	27
Cement	335	324	792	320
Ethylene & Low density Polyethylene	338	435	437	465

Electricity & Water

Electricity Generation (million KW Hour)	3549	4303	4366	4593
Water Production (million gallons)	16923	17902	17543	17543

Agriculture
(Unit of area = 1000 Donum)

Total area	11427	11427	11427	11427
Uncultivable land	11097	10777	10777	10777
Cultivable land	330	650	650	650

Main Agricultural Products
(Units in tonnes)

Cereals	1539	1977	3020	3224
Vegetables	17091	19022	19244	20927
Rootbeets	54	75	86	51
Fruit and Dates	7681	7692	8021	8404
Forage (Clover)	50303	55628	69991	72612
Red Meat & Fish	3630	3559	4388	4614
Poultry Meat	1862	1162	1500	1869
Eggs, Milk, & Dairy Production	14718	18852	20106	20023

Qatar is self-sufficient in vegetables. (*Ministry of Information and Culture*).

Livestock				
Cows	6108	7713	9422	9516
Sheep	67661	118692	121316	122529
Goats	72540	68000	86531	87396
Camels	10759	18637	22481	22706
Gazelle	2300	2415	3463	-
Foreign Trade				
Exports of Liquified Natural Gases, Butane and Propane (1000 mt)	539	652	904	796
Other basic exports				
(1000mt)	1575	1801	1703	-
Imports (Q.R. million)				
From:				
Arab Countries	340	333	360	463
E.C.	1840	1716	1575	164
Other western European countries	33	39	29	22
American countries	367	339	602	597
Asian countries	1157	1119	1173	1396
Oceania	111	135	110	150
Africa (except Arab countries)	5	4	6	7
Other countries	125	115	92	118
Government Education				
Primary Level				
Schools	92	90	89	97
Classrooms	1105	1139	1183	1260
Students	30515	31844	33306	35133
Teaching staff	2505	2764	2837	3119
Intermediate Level				
Schools	43	43	43	43
Classrooms	392	419	428	445
Students	11346.	12031	12367	12817
Teaching staff	1254	1361	1405	1469
Secondary Level				
Schools	27	25	26	29
Classrooms	271	288	293	323
Students	6915	7475	7650	8064
Teaching staff	836	889	909	1046
Specialised Education				
Schools	3	3	3	3
Classrooms	22	27	31	33
Students	581	700	856	894
Teaching staff	88	105	113	124

University Education

Universities				
Faculties	5	6	6	6
Students	4621	5057	4931	5621
University staff	401	431	452	501
Number of graduates	774	863	764	827

Qataris studying abroad

Undergraduate courses	745	679	605	512
Post graduate courses	304	287	311	333

Evening classes

Students	8072	6697	5942	6613
Primary level	4938	4335	3518	3905
Intermediate level	1795	1436	1241	1495
Secondary level	1339	1226	1183	1213

Private education

Arabic Schools				
Students	4049	5482	5034	5941
Teaching staff	205	326	309	374
Foreign Schools				
Students	9001	10537	11257	12405
Teaching staff	415	585	640	684

Health services

Hospitals	3	3	3	3
Beds	885	915	937	984
Health Centres	20	19	20	21
Doctors	437	514	560	671
Dentists	52	53	62	59
Nurses	1101	1278	1290	1341

Tourism

Luxury Hotels	4	4	4	4
Beds	1496	1458	1458	1458

Aerial view of part of the Doha corniche

Clock tower with Grand Mosque minarette.

(Ministry of Information).

MODERN QATAR

152

MODERN QATAR

Statistics however only relate part of the story. Behind Qatar's achievements in industry, education, health, and other sectors there are the people themselves, committed to meeting current challenges, deeply appreciative of the comforts and opportunities which prudent use of their oil wealth has brought them.

Careful fiscal policy has been key feature of

Above: Qatar Monetary Agency building. (*Ministry of Information and Culture*).

Opposite, top: The Qatar National Bank building with The Chartered Bank in the background. (*Ministry of Information and Culture*).

Opposite, bottom: Inside a bank vault in Doha, one is reminded of the traditionally cash nature of Qatar's economy. (*Ministry of Information and Culture*).

government. Many businessmen in Qatar derived their original income from pearl fishing, or as Bedu who profited from government contracts. Qatari entrepreneurship has flourished and today most businesses are at least 51 percent owned by Qataris. One area of business where Qatar has been particularly well endowed is that of banking with the Qatar Monetary Agency fulfilling the role Central Bank in association with six local banks and ten foreign ones. Of these Qatar National Bank is the largest. Other banks include the privately owned Commercial Bank of Qatar, the Qatar Islamic Bank, British Bank of the Middle East, Banque Paribas, Standard Chartered Bank, Gridlay's Bank, Citibank and the Arab Bank. Qatar is also base for the Gulf Organisation for Industrial Consulting.

MODERN QATAR

MODERN QATAR

Opposite, top left: Ballet dancing in Doha. (*Ministry of Information and Culture*).

Opposite, centre left: A preserved shark at Qatar National Museum where living marine life can be viewed at an excellent aquarium. (*Vine*).

Opposite, top right: Aerial view of Doha's Sheraton Hotel and surrounds. (*Ministry of Information and Culture*).

Opposite, bottom: Entrance to old Emiri palace, constructed in 1901, and in its renovated form houses one of the finest museums in the Middle East. (*Vine*).

Right and below: Lobby of Sheraton Hotel, Doha. (*Vine*).

The business traveller today will find Qatar to be an interesting and pleasant place to visit. Staying at any one of its luxury hotels: the Gulf, Sofitel, Ramada, Oasis or Sheraton, the visitor will be greeted by friendly and efficient service. Taking time out from a busy schedule of meetings, we hope that he or she will discover some aspects of the country which we have endeavoured to describe in this book. Perhaps they will take an evening stroll along the modern corniche, admiring the new Emiri Palace, the old fort and the Grand Mosque, to pause perhaps at the new national museum where one may enter the grounds of the old Emiri fort to discover a fascinating display of Qatar's past, and, through the windows of huge aquaria, admire its exotic marine environment. Further along the corniche one may pause again at the National Theatre, an elegant building, adjacent to the equally impressive Ministry of Information and Culture, and a centre for many cultural activities throughout the winter months. A stroll into the busy town of Doha may bring one, almost by accident, towards the old souk where colourful shops specialise in the sale of cloth, gold jewellery, spices, perfumes, hardware or other goods. Qatar is full of surprises and the more one explores the greater the enjoyment one is likely to experience. If time allows it pays to travel further afield outside of Doha, to the smaller, more traditional villages such as Umm Salal Mohammed, or Khor. Archaeological enthusiasts will no doubt be keen to visit Dakhira, north of Khor, which is rich in ancient remains, and of course the relatively more recent but none the less interesting deserted city of Zubara. The adjacent fort houses a unique collection of finds from the old city and these impart a feeling of closeness to the events and people who once lived along this quiet shore.

What of the future? Our account of Qatar has taken us from its earliest settlement, through prehistory, across the great rift of time since Man first fished these waters and settled upon its coastline, right up to the present where Man has learnt to harness the natural resources of the region and to create a lifestyle which will carry him forward, God willing, to the twenty-first century. While there is no doubt that the future will bring new challenges and difficulties to be overcome, it is also clear that Qatar is preparing its people to meet the demands which will be placed upon them in the years ahead.

FURTHER READING

Abu Nab, I. 1977 Qatar: a story of state building. Qatar 137pp.

Anon:- This is Qatar, Doha: Gulf Public Relations, quarterly

Arrayan, Qatar National Museum Journal, features many interesting papers on Qatar.

Bibby, G. Arabian Gulf archaeology, 1965 *Kuml* 133–152

Buckley, D.G. 1978. The excavation of seven burial cairns on the Ras Abaruk peninsula. In: *Qatar archaeological report*: excavations 1973, ed. Beatrice di Cardi: Oxford University Press.

Cavalier, C. 1970 Geological description of the Qatar peninsula. Paris: Bureau de Recherches Geologiques et Minieres, for the Government of Qatar, Department of Petroleum Affairs. 39pp.

Cottrell, A.J. 1980 The Persian Gulf States. Johns Hopkins University Press.

De Cardi, B. 1974 The British Archaeological Expedition to Qatar 1973–74. *Antiquity* (191) 48: 196–200.

Gerard, B. Qatar. Editions Delroisse.

Giob, P.V. 1959 Archaeological investigations in four Arab states. *Kuml*, 233–239.

Graham, H. 1978 Arabian Time Machine: self portrait of an oil state. Heinemann.

Harrison, D.L. 1981 Mammals of the Arabian Gulf. George Allen and Unwin.

Hawkins, D.F. 1984 Rock carvings at Al Furaihah. Arrayan 9.

Holden, D. Farewell to Arabia 1966 Faber and Faber.

Journal of the Qatar Natural History Society, no longer published.

Kapel, H. 1967 Atlas of the Stone Age cultures of Qatar. Jutland Archaeological Publications. vol. 6.

Kutschera, C. 1972 Qatar and its people. *Africa* 12, 73–78.

Lorimer, J.G. 1970 Gazeteer of the Persian Gulf, Oman, and central Arabia, Calcutta, India: Government Printing House, 1908–15. 2 vols.

Moorhead, J. 1977 In defiance of the elements: a personal view of Qatar. Quartet books.

Palgrave, W.G. 1865 Narrative of a year's journey through central and eastern Arabia (1862–63). Macmillan, reprinted by Gregg International 1969.

Qatar University Science Bulletin, published annually, commencing 1981.

Raban, J. 1979 Arabia through the looking glass. Collins.

Rice, M. 1977 National Museum of Qatar, Doha. *Museum* 29:78–87.

Sivasubramaniam, K. and M.A. Ibrahim 1982 Common Fishes of Qatar.

Smith, G.H. 1978 The stone industries of Qatar. In: *Qatar archaeological report: excavations 1973*. Edited by Beatrice de Cardi. Oxford, England: Oxford University Press. pp 35–38.

Thomas, Bertram 1932 Arabia felix: across the Empty Quarter of Arabia. Jonathon Cape.

Tibbets, G.R. 1978 Arabia in Early Maps. Oleander Press.

Vita-Finzi, C. 1978 Environmental History, in Qatar archaeological report: excavations 1973. Edited by Beatrice de Cardi. Oxford University Press.

Zahlan, R.S. 1979 The Creation of Qatar. Croom Helm. 160 pp.

ACKNOWLEDGEMENTS

We have great pleasure in thanking the many people who have helped to make this book possible. Firstly we wish to express our deepest gratitude to the Minister of Information and Culture: H.E. Sheikh Hamad bin Suhaim Al-Thani for his encouragement to us in preparation of a book of this fascinating country. We also have pleasure in thanking Abdullah Sadiq who was Director of Public Relations and Media during the period of our work on the book; and Hamad bin Thamir Al-Thani, Director of the Information Affairs Department who took an active role in guiding the project to a successful conclusion. In our work on the history of Qatar we utilised the published reports of various archaeologists who have worked in Qatar, and whom we have mentioned in the main text, and were further advised by Abdullah Al-Khulaifi, Head of Antiquities Section in the Department of Tourism and Antiquities. We are most grateful to Abdullah for his warm welcome and powerful encouragement of our efforts. Qatar's National Museum is already well known internationally as one of the finest of its kind in the Middle East. We are indebted to its Director, Darwish Mostafa Al-Far, who has helped to inspire much of the cultural appreciation for Qatar's fascinating ancient and traditional cultural heritage. In our search for additional material in this field we visited the Arab Gulf States Folklore Centre where the Director, Abdalrahman Al-Mannai, was kind enough to introduce us to his staff and to make available to us facilities of the centre. In the field of Natural History, we relied heavily upon research work carried out by staff members of the Qatar University whom we have mentioned and acknowledged in the text. We should also like to thank William Beniston who kindly offered some slides of Qatar's plantlife. We are indebted to the Acting Director of Qatar University, Dr Abdulla Juma Al Kobaisi for the open cooperation we received from all sections of the University, as well as for the interview he granted us which we have drawn upon in preparing our chapter on modern Qatar. We were particularly impressed by Qatar's vibrant artistic community and should like to thank all the artists who offered their work for publication and especially the organisers of Qatar Arts Society for their kind cooperation with this project. There are many other people and organisations who have contributed to making this book possible. We apologise for not having the space here to mention all of them but hope that they will find in these pages some acknowledgement of their contribution and will feel that their support has been worthwhile.

INDEX

ARAMCO 103
Abdu, Dr R.M. 85
Abdullah Dasman 113
Abutilon fruticosa 78
Ahmed Abdullah 109
Ahmed Zainy 127
Ahmed al Subai 124
Aizoon canariensis 77
Al Huwailah 19
Al Jussasiyah 24
Al Khalifa 23
Al Khor hill 11–13
Al Kobaisi, Dr Abdulla 140–143
Al Thani family 63
Al Wakrah 42
Alhagi maurorum 76
Ali Hassan 120
Anglo-Qatari treaty of 1868 40
Anglo-Qatari treaty of 1916 59
Ant lion 84
Armina al Minnai 111
Art and Artists 107

Badria el Khobaisi 114
Basson et al 103
Bats 105
Bibliography 156
Bird checklist 90–93
Birds 89
Blepharis ciliaris 67
Boats and boat building 53
Borj Bazann 41
Boundary agreements 62

Cistanche phelypaea 77
Climate 69
Council of Ministers 145
Cyperus conglomeratus 81

DANA offshore drilling platform 133
Demersal fish 98–99
Dipcadi erythreum 76
Dugong 104

East Indies Company 34
Education 136–138
Emir 131
Emir, H.H. Shaikh Khalifa
  bin Hamad Al Thani 63
Emiri Diwan 145
Enfield rifle 57

Facey, William 25
Falconry 64–65
Farig Idham 110
Fox 104

General Treaty of Peace, 1820 34
Geography, physical 75
Geology 70–73
Gerbil 105
Glossonema edule 76
Greek and Roman influence 16–17
Gulf Cooperation Council
  and Qatar 131

Haifa Abass
Halopeplis perfoliata 83
Hamad general Hospital 143
Hare 104
Hassan Sultan Juman Naimi 64–65
Hassan al Mulla 126
Head of State 131
Hedgehog 104
Hissa el Merikh 112
History 11
Hotels 155
Hydrography 96

Insect fauna, checklist 86
Insects 85
International influence in Gulf,
  16th & 17th cent. 19
Internecine strife: 1874–1891 42–44
Isa bin Tarif 40–42
Islam 17

Jemila Sherim 46
Jeroba 105

Kassite period 15
Khor Al Udeid 68
Khor Hill 11
Khor island 19

Limonium axillare 83
Lizards 94
Lorimer 34
Lycium shawii 81

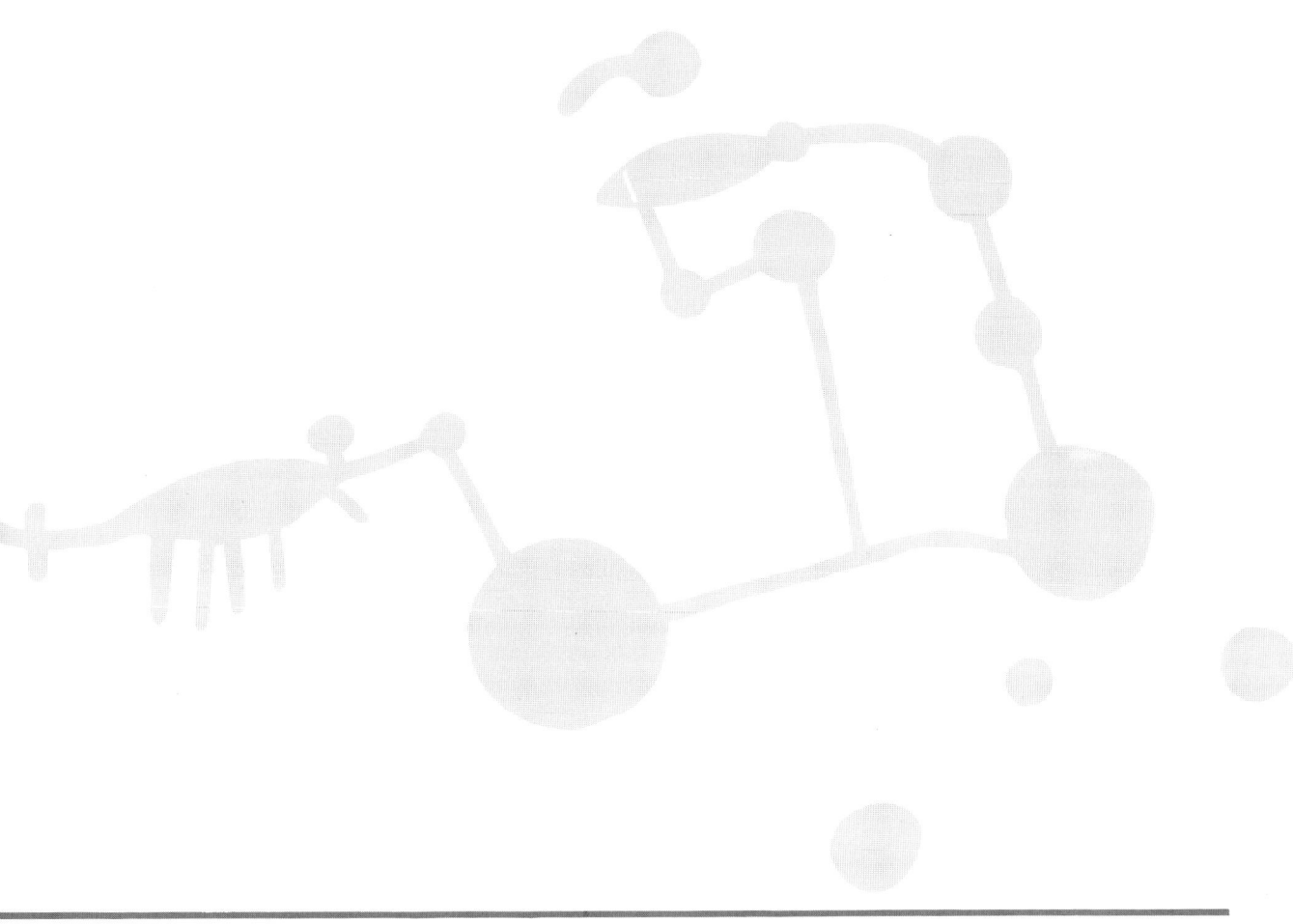

Maged Hilal 121
Mammals 103
Maps 8–9
Margid Hilal 46
Mariam Mohammed 119
Marine life 95
Mesopotamian influence 14–15
Modern Qatar 131
Mohammed Ali Abdullah 123
Mohammed al Jida 122
Mohammed, Dr M.B.H. 94
Murwab 19

Naged al Sulaiti 125
National theatre 155
Natural gas 133
Natural history 67
Nearchos and Alexander's routes 16–17
Neolithic 11
Niebuhr, Carsten 23
North Field 131

Oil concession and protection agreements: 1935 60
Oryx, scimitar horned 104
Ottoman presence, 1871 43

Pearl oysters 102
Pearling industry 49–51
Pearls, trade 52–53
Pelagic fish 101
Pelly, Col. 41

Perpetual Maritime truce, 1832-1853
Plants 77

QAFCO 134
QAPCO 134
QASCO 134
Qatar General Petroleum Corporation 131
Qatar National Petroleum Company 131
Qatar Television 143
Qatar University 135

Rahmah ibn Jabir 29, 36–37
Ras al Khaimah 35
Rashid al Mohannadi 116–117
Reptiles 94
Rock art 24–26

Sabkhas 82
Sasanid empire 17
Sea cow 104
Sea creatures 96
Seleucids 16–17
Senecio sp. 76
Sergeant 18
Shagra 11
Shaikh Qasim defeats Turks 45
Shrimps 101
Snakes 94
Souk, traditional in Doha 58–59
Statistics 146–153
Stone Age 11

Telecommunications 143
Traditional life 46
Transition years, 1832–47 39
Turkish claims to Qatar 44
Turtles 94

Ubaid period 11–12
Umm Suwayjah 35
Umm Said 133
Utbi 23

Wafiga Sultan 115

Yaqut al Hamawi 18
Yousef Ahmed 128, 129

Zgain al Bahth 19
Ziziphus nummularia 78
Zubara, artifacts 28, 30
Zubara, colonisation in 1766 20
Zubara, fort 32
Zubara, ruins 20–21
Zubara, seige of 29
Zubara, turmoil 1766–1782 27–28
Zygophyllum qatarense 83